GOOD SPORTS

Plain Talk About Health and Fitness for Teens

Nissa Simon

Illustrations by Patricia Tobin

THOMAS Y. CROWELL   NEW YORK

I'd like to thank:

Donald Bagnall, A.T., C., head athletic trainer at the
Hopkins School, New Haven, Connecticut, who gener-
ously took time from his busy schedule to read the manu-
script and offer valuable suggestions.

My editor, Marc Aronson, for his confidence, support,
and helpful editing.

My children—Rob, Jonea, and Andrea Gurwitt—who
knew just when to ask how it's going and when to steal
silently from the room. No writer (or mother) could ask
for more.

And above all, Melvin Woody—who makes it all possible.

Good Sports: Plain Talk About Health and Fitness for Teens
Text copyright © 1990 by Nissa Simon
Illustrations copyright © 1990 by Patricia Tobin
Printed in the United States of America.
For information address Thomas Y. Crowell Junior Books,
10 East 53rd Street, New York, NY 10022.
1   2   3   4   5   6   7   8   9   10
First Edition

Library of Congress Cataloging-in-Publication Data
Simon, Nissa.
    Good sports : plain talk about health and fitness for teens / by
  Nissa Simon ; illustrations by Patricia Tobin.
       p.   cm.
    Summary: Basic health and fitness information includes nutrition
  and exercise tips, as well as a section on sports injuries.
    ISBN 0-690-04902-1. —ISBN 0-690-04904-8 (lib. bdg.)
    1. Pediatric sports medicine.   2. Physical fitness.   3. Youth—
  Health and hygiene.   [1. Physical fitness.   2. Health.   3. Sports
  medicine.]   I. Title.
  RC1218.C45S55   1990   89-78556
  613'.0433—dc20   CIP
                                                                        AC

For Melvin, with love

Contents

Introduction *vii*

1 Fitness *1*

2 Before Starting *8*

3 Nutrition for the Sports-Conscious Teenager *17*

4 Warming Up and Cooling Down *29*

5 Stretching *35*

6 The Psychological Side of Sports *44*

7 Common Physical Problems *53*

8 Lower-Body Injuries *60*

9 Upper-Body Injuries *74*

10 Weather Extremes and Exercise *84*

11 Drugs *93*

Special Terms *105*

Index *111*

Introduction

More than 2,500 years ago, Greek athletes trained rigor-
ously for sports contests. Indeed, the Greeks thought
sports so important that they based their whole calendar
on the four-year intervals between Olympic games and
even stopped all wars whenever the games were due.
The contests included running, leaping, discus throwing,
wrestling, and boxing. The Greeks understood the importance of regular practice and professional training. In
addition to practicing for their events, athletes were
taught to carry heavy loads, lift weights, and bend iron
rods. And, even then, coaches considered diet an essential part of the training regimen. At the ancient equivalent of the training table, athletes ate fresh cheese, dried
figs, and bread.

Since those ancient times, sports have changed. New
games have been introduced, and athletes themselves
have improved. They break records regularly. In 1896,
the year the ancient games were revived, the men's

Olympic marathon record was 2:58:50. By 1988, Olympic winners had knocked more than forty-eight minutes off that time. In 1912, the first year women competed, the winner of the women's 100-meter freestyle swimming competition clocked in at 1:22.2. The 1988 winner bettered that record by a third, finishing in 54.93.

In part, these improvements can be explained by more practice time and better nutrition. But modern training techniques and better methods of physical conditioning have probably made the most difference. As a teenager, you may not understand how to apply these techniques to improve your own performance—or even know where to get the information in the first place.

If you take up any sport, even casually, you'll want to know how to avoid injuries—and how to treat them if they do occur. What do you do for a charley horse? How do you deal with a blister? Where can you find out about proper nutrition or the elements of fitness? What about drugs? Do they help or hurt your performance?

This book gives you correct information, based on the most recent research, about all these subjects. It also tells you about warming up and cooling down—and how to exercise safely in hot and cold weather. The book explains the physical reasons for proper training practices and what can happen if you ignore them. The chapter on nutrition tells you not only what to eat and what not to eat, but why you should ignore some of the old nutrition myths. The chapter on common physical problems explains what to do about a stitch in your side, as well as the difference between sprains and strains. But it isn't enough to know how to avoid a sprain. There's far more to sports than physical concerns—so the book includes discussions of the psychological aspects of sports, and the ever-mounting problem of drugs in sports.

The book is organized to lead the reader from preparation for healthy competition to how to deal with risks and injuries. The first six chapters explain the basic concepts of fitness and training, and the next five discuss specific physical problems, how to avoid them, and how to treat them if they do occur.

Of course, this book is no substitute for professional advice. If you have questions that aren't covered here, you can ask your coach. But, it's not a coach's job to keep track of the latest developments in health or medicine, so a coach may not be right every time. If the advice doesn't seem right to you, trust your own judgment. When in doubt, see a doctor. Remember, it's your body.

Some readers may not read the book straight through because they are likely to come to it with some special question or concern—or in search of information on a particular topic. The book is arranged to make it easy to find the answers to such specific questions. The book also contains a list of terms along with an explanation of each.

This book is written for both young men and young women, since both now compete in almost every sport. Because it's awkward to repeat "he or she" and "his or her" in each sentence, where necessary I have used one or the other, but I mean to refer to both, except where the information is sex specific.

CHAPTER 1

Fitness

For a lot of teenagers, being fit or being in shape means having a body that looks good to other people. That's why some teenagers lift weights or work out on machines. But weight lifters may not be able to run a mile or do somersaults. Are they fit? Just what does fitness mean?

If you think about how sports differ from each other, you'll see that fitness means something different in each sport. Being fit to run a marathon and being fit to compete in a diving competition aren't the same kind of fitness. Being fit to play in a baseball game and being fit to last out a soccer match aren't the same kind of fitness either.

Participating in sports doesn't automatically get you in shape. Truly fit athletes rarely get in shape by playing their sport. They get in shape first to play their sport. In other words, they don't play to get fit, they get fit to play.

Of course, just as we speak about all-around athletes,

1

we can speak of all-around fitness. Being physically fit is more than being able to drive in runs or lift weights or make baskets. Fitness isn't a single skill or strength, it's a combination of several different ingredients. Cardiovascular endurance, muscle endurance (stamina), muscle strength, flexibility, and weight control all contribute to physical fitness.

You can develop each of these through exercise—and some athletes do. But being fit and being an athlete are not the same thing. For instance, runners generally have well-developed cardiovascular endurance, but not well-developed upper body strength. Weight lifters have incredible muscle strength, but little cardiovascular endurance. Baseball players have specific muscle endurance, but generally lack cardiovascular endurance. To be truly fit, you must condition your heart and lungs to work at their best, strengthen your muscles and develop them so they can repeat a movement, stretch your tendons and ligaments, and weigh neither too much nor too little. To be truly fit, you must develop all the components of fitness, not just one or two. Just what do these separate components of fitness fit you for?

Cardiovascular Endurance

Most people think first of muscle strength when they think of fitness, but in fact the most important ingredient is cardiovascular endurance. To be able to skip rope or swim for half an hour, your heart must be able to pump oxygen-rich blood to your muscles. Cardiovascular endurance is the ability of your heart, lungs, and circulatory system to work together to deliver oxygen to your body's cells and to take away waste products. Without satisfactory cardiovascular endurance, your performance will fall off in almost any sport.

To build up cardiovascular endurance, you have to condition your heart and lungs to work more efficiently. You can do this through aerobic ("with air") exercises. Activities that require continuous movement and raise your pulse rate, such as running, swimming, or cycling, are the best way to build up heart and lung stamina. These aerobic exercises improve the ability of your heart and lungs to deliver oxygen to your muscles more efficiently.

Muscle Endurance and Muscle Strength

In order for an offensive lineman to move a defender out of the way, he needs muscle strength. A figure skater needs muscle endurance to complete a routine. But without both—muscle strength and muscle endurance— neither of these athletes will be able to work at peak level. To do well in sports, you need both muscle strength and muscle endurance. Strength is the greatest force a muscle can produce—once. Endurance is the ability to repeat the movement again and again. Muscle strength and endurance are closely related, yet distinct. And you develop them by different kinds of exercise.

3

You develop strength by lifting a heavy weight a few times, but you build endurance by lifting a lighter weight many times.

You can build up muscle strength with strength training, also called progressive resistance training. When you exercise your muscles by lifting weights that are near the maximum you can lift, your muscles increase in size. You'll develop stronger, more efficient muscles.

Strong muscles help prevent injuries. In fact, this is one of the main goals of strength training. Time and again, coaches find that an injured athlete who's on a conditioning/strength training program recovers more quickly and loses fewer days of practice than one who isn't.

You can build muscle endurance by repetition, working *below* your maximum level but increasing the number of repetitions.

Athletes need different kinds of endurance for different sports. Short-term endurance is needed in sports where bursts of intense activity last only a few seconds, such as football. Long-term endurance is needed for sports that require extended muscle exertion for longer periods, such as cross-country skiing. But whatever the sport, general endurance conditioning is important.

Sit-ups, push-ups, and chin-ups are all good exercises to build endurance; so are running and cycling. The key to endurance training is to build up the number of times you can repeat an exercise or the distance you cycle or run.

4

Flexibility

It's hard to imagine a gymnast who isn't flexible. A stiff, musclebound gymnast wouldn't last long on the bars or rings, but would end up in an ungainly sprawl on the floor. Flexibility allows athletes to move gracefully—but it does more than that. Flexible joints and muscles help to protect against injuries. Athletes who are not flexible are more likely to strain muscles or injure joints.

Flexibility is the range of movement of your muscles and joints. If you can't touch your toes without bending your knees, your lower back and legs aren't as flexible as they should be. If you can't do a backward somersault, your back needs limbering. You can develop more flexible muscles and joints by including gentle stretching exercises in your warm-up routine. Remember to warm up your body with gentle jogging or cycling before you start stretching. Cold muscles are more easily injured than warm ones.

Weight Control

Your body actually needs some fat to store energy, protect your internal organs, and insulate you from the cold. But your body doesn't need too much fat—that just slows you down. Football players and wrestlers look big because they carry around a lot of muscle—but not much fat. Swimmers, gymnasts, and runners all have well-developed muscles and lean bodies. Teenagers who compete in sports regularly develop their muscles—and keep their fat under control.

How much is too much? Teenage boys should have an average of 7 percent to 12 percent of their weight as fat, and teenage girls should have about 15 percent to 18 percent of their weight as fat. But how do you find out how much fat you have?

A precise way of measuring body fat is to be weighed under water in a specially designed tank. Not too many high-school gyms are equipped with these tanks, however. A simpler way to determine the amount of body fat is to use skin calipers to measure skin-fold thickness. Your coach probably knows how to take these measurements. If not, you can get a rough measure by standing straight and pinching the skin at your waistline between your thumb and index finger. If your fingers are spread more than an inch apart, you're probably carrying around too much fat.

"No Pain, No Gain"

Unfortunately, teenagers who compete in intramural or intermural sports often assume that training principles meant for competitive athletes apply to them. One such principle that's caused a great deal of mischief is "No pain, no gain," a slogan frequently posted on high-school locker room walls.

Professional athletes in top form often train at maximum strength and endurance. In order to increase their strength and become even more fit, they progressively force their muscles to do more work than they're used to—a principle known as progressive overload. These intense workouts generally cause sharp pain during exercise (often called "the burn") that disappears afterwords. Although injury is the usual cause of pain, the pain of the burn is caused by inadequate circulation. When you contract a muscle, the pressure reduces blood flow, and there's not enough oxygen to meet the muscle's need. When you relax, oxygen-supplying blood rushes into the muscle, relieving the pain.

Professional athletes often believe that they must work through the burn to achieve maximum muscle growth. But training with pain is often harmful, not helpful, to nonprofessional athletes. If you train to the point of pain and exhaustion, you're likely to become nauseated, dizzy, and unable to continue working out. Unless you're an elite, professional athlete, "no pain, no gain" makes no sense. You can maintain a steady level of fitness without persistent pain.

To do well in your sport, you must be truly fit—and there's no mystery about how to go about it. Work to develop all the elements of fitness—not just one or two—so they act together.

CHAPTER 2

Before Starting

Different sports use different muscles and use them differently. To train for each sport requires specific exercises. But you need more than muscles to perform at your peak. You also need energy.

Aerobic and Anaerobic Exercise

You use energy if you sprint in a dash or run in a marathon—but you use a distinct kind of energy for each activity.

Your body has two systems that supply energy: anaerobic ("without air") and aerobic ("with air"). The anaerobic system provides immediate energy for sudden, intense activity. The aerobic system delivers oxygen for prolonged activity.

Your heart pumps oxygen-rich blood to every cell in your body, your cells use the oxygen to provide energy, and your blood carries away the resulting waste products.

To build up your cardiovascular endurance, you must build up your heart's ability to carry oxygen-rich blood throughout your body. You can do this through aerobic exercise.

When you first start to exercise, or when you need a sudden burst of energy, your muscles function anaerobically (without oxygen). Sports such as sprinting, baseball, or football that require short bursts of energy and long pauses between them use the anaerobic system. But if you exercise continuously and strenuously for more than two or three minutes, your muscles need fresh oxygen to produce enough energy to keep you going. You take in the needed oxygen through your lungs, and your heart pumps it throughout your body. Aerobic exercise builds up your body's ability to bring in more oxygen.

If you keep exercising strenuously, you'll reach a point where your lungs and heart can't supply enough oxygen to rid your body of waste, which builds up in the form of a chemical called lactic acid. Lactic acid interferes with efficient muscle function and causes fatigue. The more you push yourself, the more exhausted you become. You've crossed over the point called the "anaerobic threshold"; your feelings of fatigue are nature's way of telling you to slow down and cut back your level of activity. However, you can raise the point at which you reach your anaerobic threshold by increasing your body's maximum aerobic capacity.

To improve your aerobic condition, you have to increase your heart's capacity to pump blood by pushing your heart to between 60 percent and 80 percent of its

9

maximum rate during exercise—and sustaining the increased rate during the exercise session. This rate is called your target heart rate. To determine your target heart rate, subtract your age from 220. (For instance, if you're 16 years old, 220 − 16 = 204.) Multiply that figure by 60, 70, or 80 percent (for example, 204 × .80 = 163). That's the training heart rate, in beats per minute, you should work up to.

With continued training, your heart pumps more strongly and beats less frequently to circulate the same amount of blood so, as you become more fit, you'll be able to increase the amount of exercise that elevates your heart rate to its target rate.

To achieve the benefits of aerobic conditioning, plan on exercising for twenty to forty minutes at least three or four times a week. But concentrating on one kind of exercise for that length of time can get boring. To add interest and to improve overall conditioning, coaches sometimes recommend a method of training called interval training. Interval training emphasizes different kinds of exercises during a single workout, usually weight lifting combined with some kind of aerobic workout.

You'll need a good aerobic foundation for all sports so that you can get through long practices and games without fatigue. Bicycling, swimming, skipping rope, rowing, and race walking are all good aerobic exercises. You can train anaerobically with any activity that demands a short, intense burst of energy, such as sprinting, ski jumping, or weight lifting.

Muscles

You can't move without muscles. Muscles enable you to lift your arm to raise a tennis racket or bend your knees at the starting block. Muscles make it possible to turn your eyes from side to side, to move your jaw to chew food, and to digest food once you've swallowed it.

To understand about building up your muscles through exercise, it's important to understand how muscles work.

Your body contains more than four hundred muscles—including your heart, a muscle that pumps blood. Even the walls of your stomach are lined with muscles, which are called "involuntary" because they operate whether you will them to or not.

The kind of muscles you use in sports and train through exercise are called "voluntary" muscles because you can voluntarily control their movement. Some of these voluntary muscles are attached to tendons that anchor them to bones. These are called skeletal muscles. Skeletal muscles make up about 40 percent of your weight. Under a microscope, skeletal muscle fiber looks striped, so another name for them is striped, or "striated," muscle.

Each muscle contains thousands of cells, called muscle fibers, bundled together and wrapped in connective tissue. Nerves link these fibers to the brain. When you want to move your arm or leg, or use any voluntary muscle, your brain sends a nerve impulse that causes the muscle to contract (shorten) or relax. Most muscles work in pairs; when one contracts, the opposing muscle relaxes. When you bend your arm, for example, nerve impulses reach the fibers of the biceps (the muscle in your upper arm) causing it to contract; as it contracts, the opposing muscle, the triceps, relaxes and the arm bends. When you want to straighten your arm, nerve impulses cause the triceps to contract; as this happens, the biceps relaxes and your arm straightens.

These paired muscles are called the agonist and antagonist. When you bend your arm, the biceps is the agonist, because it contracts, and the triceps is the antagonist, because it relaxes. When you want to straighten your arm, the muscles reverse roles and the biceps becomes the antagonist, the triceps the agonist. Happily, you don't have to think of each muscle's action separately when you want to bend your arm because the muscle teams work together, using a common nerve for their related actions.

Types of Exercise

All exercises fall under one of three basic categories: isometric, isotonic, and isokinetic.

An isometric exercise contracts and relaxes a muscle group with no movement; one such exercise is pushing your hands together as hard as you can. Isometric exercises increase muscle strength. An isotonic exercise contracts and relaxes muscle groups through movement against resistance; examples would be lifting free weights or doing push-ups. Isotonic exercises increase the ability of the heart to pump blood and the lungs to absorb oxygen. An isokinetic exercise is an isotonic exercise in which a specialized exercise machine provides accommodating resistance—that is, resistance can be varied to accommodate changing levels of strength.

Different sports and exercises call different kinds of skeletal muscle fibers into play. Speed and strength rest primarily in "fast-twitch" fibers, also called Type II fibers. Muscular endurance depends upon "slow-twitch," or Type I, fibers.

Muscular strength and muscular endurance are interrelated. You need endurance to run the length of the field with a football. You need strength to kick the ball over the goalposts for a field goal.

By contracting intensely and forcefully, fast-twitch fibers provide rapid movement for short periods of time. They also tire quickly. Muscles such as the calves, biceps, and triceps are made up mostly of fast-twitch fibers. These fibers provide the speed and force necessary for sprinting, jumping, and throwing, which all require intense bursts of effort.

Slow-twitch fibers contract slowly and with less force, but tire less quickly. Slow-twitch fibers are important for endurance sports such as long-distance running and cross-country skiing. Slow-twitch fibers also help you stand straight and maintain your posture.

You can actually see the difference between the two types of fiber under a microscope. Fast-twitch fibers work anaerobically; they are white. Slow-twitch fibers work aerobically; they are supplied with oxygen through a network of blood vessels, so they are red.

Heredity determines the proportion of fast-twitch to slow-twitch fibers. You're born with more of one kind of these fibers than the other and you can't change one type to the other through training. But you can change the fiber's characteristics. Through strength-training exercises, you can substantially increase the size of fast-twitch fibers and slightly increase the size of slow-twitch fibers. Through endurance training you can increase the ability of slow-twitch fibers to use oxygen. That's why different kinds of exercises are necessary to prepare for sports — and your training program will differ depending on the sport.

You can build strength best with strength training, also known as progressive resistance training. These exercises not only increase the size of your muscles, but help to develop stronger, more efficient ones. Once you start getting stronger, you'll also have more stamina and speed. When you increase the strength of a muscle, you also increase its speed of movement. The result is more power—strength combined with speed—which makes you faster. Strength training will also make you less susceptible to injuries by strengthening your muscles, ligaments, and tendons.

When you repeatedly lift near the maximum amount of weight you can lift, the resistance "overloads" the muscles—that is, they contract at close to maximum tension and increase in size and strength. The increase in size is called hypertrophy. Hypertrophy results from an increase in the diameter of the individual muscle fibers that make up the muscles. Some researchers believe that the muscle grows by "splitting" under the strain and "healing" after the workout by adding protein. In untrained muscles, the diameter of the fibers varies. With training, the diameter of the small fibers increases to the size of the larger ones.

Girls sometimes worry that strength training will develop overlarge muscles. But it won't—for two reasons. One, the male hormone testosterone partly controls hypertrophy, so the same exercise won't make a girl's muscle as large as a boy's. And two, although the composition of muscle fiber for boys and girls is similar, muscle fiber size also affects hypertrophy, and boys' muscle fiber is larger.

When you exercise to build strength, you'll get the most benefit from heavy resistance and few repetitions of the full cycle of exercises. Lift no more weight than you can comfortably handle in twelve repetitions before you get tired. When you train, do four to twelve repetitions (one set) for each group of muscles. Repeat each set no more than three times a day and don't work on the same muscles more than three days a week. To lessen the chance of overuse injuries, use less weight and high repetitions. Because muscles need enough time to recover between workouts, lift weights or use the machines one day and rest the next. If you don't, your muscles won't recuperate; they'll become weaker, not stronger.

Coaches often design routines around core exercises, those that develop large muscle groups such as those in the shoulders, hips, buttocks, and thighs or in the abdominal area. Typical core lifts include the squat (to develop leg and hip strength), power clean (to develop explosive power), and bench press (to build upper-body strength). They add auxiliary exercises to these routines to strengthen muscles for particular sports. Volleyball players, for instance, must strengthen leg muscles for jumping, and tennis players must stress exercises that develop arm and shoulder muscles. A well-balanced routine includes at least one core exercise for the lower body, one for the upper body, and half a dozen or so additional exercises.

To build endurance, by contrast, the key is repetition without heavy resistance. Work below your maximum level and slowly increase the number of sit-ups, push-ups, or chin-ups, for instance. You can also use light free weights or dumbbells to develop upper-body muscle endurance.

Playing basketball develops one set of muscles, bicycling develops another—but strength training develops a range of muscles. And strength training paired with aerobic exercise builds muscle strength and endurance in a way that no single exercise can.

CHAPTER 3

Nutrition for the Sports-Conscious Teenager

A determined athlete always looks for a way to improve performance, whether it's carrying a lucky charm or eating a magic diet. And even though there's some reason to suppose that high-level performance is fueled by what we eat, there's no magic diet that will make you a winner every time.

Knowing what to eat and what not to eat is as basic to performing well as knowing how to exercise and when to stop. But it's easy to be confused by all the conflicting claims about special foods and fad diets. Good nutrition for anyone involved in sports follows the same basics as good nutrition for everyone: a balanced diet with foods chosen from a variety of sources.

We all need to get certain basic substances called nutrients from food. Five of these nutrients are essential to life: proteins, carbohydrates, fats, vitamins, and minerals.

• PROTEIN provides the building blocks for every part of your body except fat. Meats, eggs, cheese, fish, beans, soy, lentils, breads, and cereals all contain protein.

- CARBOHYDRATES provide the body's most readily available source of energy. Carbohydrates are starches and sugars that are digested rapidly and converted to glucose (commonly called "blood sugar"). Glucose is used for energy or stored in muscle tissue and the liver in the form of glycogen. When you need energy, your body reconverts glycogen to glucose. If you don't eat enough carbohydrates to provide the glucose you need for energy, your body will instead use protein that should be used to build and repair muscle. Rice, fruits, potatoes, beans, corn, and other vegetables are all carbohydrate-rich foods.

- FAT provides energy and helps with the absorption of the fat-soluble vitamins: A, D, E, and K. When fat is digested, it carries these vitamins along into your bloodstream. After fat reaches the bloodstream, some is burned as energy; the rest is stored, to be used in the future.

- VITAMINS are organic substances not manufactured by the body. Vitamins help to convert food to living tissue, and help the body utilize the energy in food.

- MINERALS are inorganic compounds that contribute to energy production and body maintenance.

How can you make sure you're eating the food you need for peak performance? By eating a balanced diet. Each day, your diet should include four servings of a dairy food (milk, cheese, yogurt, cottage cheese), two servings of a protein food (meat or poultry, fish, eggs, dried beans and peas, peanut butter, cheese), four serv-

18

ings of fruits and vegetables, and four servings of grains (pasta, bread, cereal, rice). In addition, you need three tablespoons of some kind of fat each day, which you can get from mayonnaise, salad dressing, butter, or oil.

Most foods contain a combination of these nutrients. Milk, for instance, is rich in calcium, a mineral, but also contains vitamins A and D, carbohydrates, and fat. Spaghetti, a good source of carbohydrates, also provides protein. A slice of cheese pizza is rich in protein and carbohydrates, but also provides vitamin A, calcium, and fat.

All foods also contain calories. But what is a calorie? Most people tend to think of calories as a measure of potential fat, but calories are really a measure of potential energy. A calorie is a way of measuring the amount of energy (in the form of heat) that the body can produce from a food substance. When food is digested, the body uses it as fuel to generate energy. If you eat more food than you burn to provide energy, the extra potential energy is stored in the form of fat—ready to be used if needed.

Simply choosing foods from these basic food groups won't automatically guarantee that you're eating a balanced diet, however. For example, carbohydrates come in two forms. Foods such as rice, grain, vegetables, and fruit contain unrefined carbohydrates. These foods also contain rich amounts of vitamins and minerals, and not too many calories. Candy, sugar, jams, and syrups contain refined carbohydrates. Refining mechanically strips away bulk and nutrients, leaving a concentrated sugar or starch. Foods high in refined carbohydrates, such as candy and cakes, also tend to have a lot of fat—and a lot of calories. These foods are said to contain "empty calories," because they supply very few of the necessary nutrients.

Many teenagers eat large amounts of red meat because they think that a high-protein diet improves performance. That's probably the oldest training-table myth around. The truth is that strenuous physical activity doesn't increase your protein requirements. It does increase the amount of calories you need—and these calories should come from all sources. Although muscles are made up of protein, exercise doesn't deplete protein or break down muscles, nor will protein supplements make muscles stronger. Indeed, excess protein doesn't turn into muscle, it turns into fat.

A pregame meal that features a big steak will probably cut down your performance rather than improve it. Here's how: During digestion, your body breaks down proteins into smaller units called amino acids, which contain nitrogen. These amino acids are carried first to the liver. From there, they disperse to other cells in the body to build new proteins. If you eat more protein than you need, your liver removes the nitrogen from the amino acids and converts it to uric acid, and your kidneys excrete it in urine. Doubling or tripling the amount of protein you eat won't supply it to your muscles. Instead, you'll only make extra work for your liver and kidneys.

Regular exercise tailored to specific muscle groups *and* more calories will increase muscle size and strength, but the calories must come from protein, carbohydrates, and fat—not just protein.

How much protein is enough? If you're interested in numbers, here they are: In general, girls should eat 46 grams of protein a day; boys between eleven and fourteen years old should eat 45 grams of protein a day, and boys between fifteen and eighteen years old should eat 56 grams of protein a day. There's no easy way to count the grams of protein you eat, so look at how much there is in some ordinary food. A glass of skim milk has 9 grams of protein, one chicken drumstick has 12 grams, two tablespoons of peanut butter have 8 grams, and a quarter pound of beef has 23 grams.

Of course, you're not going to sit down and add up the grams of protein in the food you're about to eat—and there's no need to. If you eat a reasonable diet, it's hard not to get enough protein. Almost any athlete's diet probably has more than enough protein.

Instead of wolfing down red meat, it's much more important to eat enough complex carbohydrates. Your body converts carbohydrates into glucose. Then various systems in your body convert the glucose into glycogen, which is stored in muscles and liver. If your muscle glycogen stores drop too low, you'll feel tired and won't be able to exercise efficiently. To work at your peak, emphasize carbohydrates in your daily diet. Sixty percent of your daily calories should come from complex carbohydrates such as whole-grain breads, pasta, vegetables, and fruits; the remaining calories should come from equal proportions of protein and fat.

Most athletes who train for endurance events such as marathons often practice a special technique called carbohydrate loading. They deliberately pack their muscle glycogen stores before an event—greatly increasing their endurance. Normal stores of glycogen last for up to two hours of continuous hard exercise. Once they're used up, you become exhausted and must either stop exercising or slow down. Carbohydrate loading enables athletes to keep going for three hours or longer. If your event is shorter than ninety minutes, carbohydrate loading won't help. It doesn't increase your pace, but enables you to hold out for more than two hours.

A lot of people think that carbohydrate loading means eating a spaghetti dinner a couple of hours before the event. But it's more complicated than that. Until recently, the theory held that you could build up glycogen stores only after depleting them. So athletes who wanted to "load" their muscles would first eat a *low*-carbohydrate diet before attempting to rebuild glycogen stores, a technique that made them dizzy, tired, and nauseated. Because of these side effects, some specialists stressed that athletes should use carbohydrate loading only for an occasional endurance event. Others believed that carbohydrate loading should be used only by professional athletes under strict supervision.

We now know it isn't necessary to first deplete glycogen stores in order to build them up. A combination of tapering your training and increasing carbohydrates in your diet for the week before an endurance event works just as well. Here's how to do it:

During the week before the event, gradually taper off the amount of endurance exercise. Six days before the event, exercise hard for ninety minutes and eat meals that supply about half of their calories from carbohydrates. For the next two days, continue eating the same amount of carbohydrates, but cut down exercise to forty minutes. On the following two days, cut down exercise even further—to twenty minutes. Too much exercise at this point will use up the stored glycogen. During these two days, increase carbohydrates in your diet to about 70 percent of calories. For instance, instead of a second piece of chicken at dinner, take a second baked potato. The day before the event, don't exercise at all (except for stretching), but continue eating high-carbohydrate meals.

Figuring out your diet isn't hard. First, here are some sample serving sizes from the different food groups: A serving from the dairy group—one glass of milk or one and a half slices of Swiss or cheddar cheese; from the protein group—a piece of chicken or a small hamburger; from the fruit and vegetable group—an apple, a half cup of broccoli, or a glass of orange juice; and from the grain group—one slice of bread or a half cup of spaghetti.

For the first three days, when you eat meals that supply half of their calories from carbohydrates, each day eat four servings from the fruit and vegetable group, four servings from the grain group, and two servings each from the dairy and protein groups. During the next three days, when you increase the amount of carbohydrates to about 70 percent of calories, each day eat two servings each from the dairy and protein groups, eight servings of

23

fruits and vegetables, and twelve servings from the grain group.

Here's a sample day's worth of meals that contain about 2,500 calories, 70 percent of them from carbohydrates, the rest from protein and fat:

Breakfast. An orange, a cup of cornflakes topped with a sliced banana, two slices of toast with butter or margarine, and a glass of low-fat milk.

Lunch. A turkey sandwich with a slice of cheese, lettuce and tomato salad, a glass of low-fat milk, and an apple.

Dinner. Two cups of spaghetti with tomato sauce and grated cheese, two slices of bread, string beans, half a grapefruit.

Snacks. Popcorn, no butter.

Three to five hours before the event eat a 500- to 800-calorie carbohydrate-rich meal without much fat or bulk. One good meal would include a glass of orange juice, a piece of white-bread toast with jelly, and a glass of low-fat milk. Or, if you want, you could substitute a bowl of Cream of Wheat or a serving of spaghetti for the toast.

Carbohydrate loading only works if you're already fit and trained for endurance sports. If you're not, your muscles can't store any more glycogen than usual.

Carbohydrate loading does not mean filling up on the empty calories of cakes, soft drinks, and cookies. If you eat these empty-calorie foods, you'll short-change yourself of vitamins and minerals necessary for good health. Eat fruits, vegetables, and whole grains; they provide nutrients along with calories.

And don't just reach for a candy bar before an event in hopes that it will provide a burst of quick energy. Actually, it will do just the opposite. To cope with the large amount of sugar in a candy bar, your pancreas has to pour out insulin and your blood sugar goes down. In turn, your body will use up glycogen stores to raise blood sugar—and you'll tire sooner. In addition, the concentrated sugar in a candy bar holds fluids in the stomach and small intestine, which may cause nausea, cramps, and dehydration.

It's also important to drink a lot of water when you exercise or compete. The loss of body fluid through sweating can affect your performance. But worse than that, you can become seriously dehydrated or suffer from heat exhaustion. For instance, during competition, marathon runners can lose as much as 8 percent of their body weight through sweating. Other athletes may sweat away 2 percent to 4 percent of their weight. If you weigh 150 pounds and lose 4 percent of your weight through sweating, you've lost six pounds of water—roughly three quarts.

Don't count on thirst to tell you when your body needs water. While you're exercising strenuously or competing in a game, your body will lose about three pounds of fluid before you feel thirsty. Even when you finally do feel thirsty, you won't drink as much as you need. Typically, athletes who rely on thirst only drink two thirds of the fluid they need. To see how much fluid you lose during training, weigh yourself both before and after exercise. You should drink one pint of fluid (two full glasses) for each pound you lost during exercise. To make sure you get enough fluid, drink water before, during, and after exercise. Drink two glasses of water before you start exercising, one glass every fifteen minutes during exercise, and two glasses when you finish.

Contrary to popular belief, you won't get stomach cramps if you drink cold water. Cold water is better for you than tepid water—for two reasons. Cold water helps to keep your body cool because you use body heat to warm it, lowering your body temperature. Also, the body can absorb water only through the small intestine, and cold fluids pass from the stomach to the small intestine more quickly than warm ones.

The best exercise drink is plain cold water. Commercial drinks formulated to replace lost minerals can cause stomach cramps because of the amount of sugar they contain. You don't need the electrolytes (potassium, sodium, phosphorus, and chlorine) in these drinks to replace the minerals lost in sweat. You'll replace them easily anyway—during your next meal. And you don't need salt tablets either unless your doctor advises you to take them. You can replace the small amount of salt you lose in sweat with a handful of salted potato chips.

When you eat may be as important to high performance as *what* you eat.

When you eat, your heart pumps blood to your stomach and small intestine to help digest the food. If you begin to exercise before the food is digested, your muscles compete for the blood—and your muscles win. Di-

26

gestion stops, and you'll feel bloated and possibly crampy. You're more likely to get cramps or feel bloated if you eat foods high in fat or protein before you exercise. Fat and protein are digested more slowly than carbohydrate and stay in your digestive tract longer. They also tend to increase blood acidity level—and a high acid level is associated with fatigue. It takes between three and four hours to digest a large meal, between an hour and a half and two hours to digest a light meal. Wait until then before you exercise.

Although timing the meals you eat after the game or practice isn't critical, you can replace glycogen by eating large helpings of complex carbohydrates such as potatoes, pasta, or rice soon after you exercise. But it will take a day or two to completely replenish your muscle glycogen stores.

Many teenage athletes tend to skip breakfast because there's no time, they're on a diet, or they're not hungry. But a reasonable breakfast is a simple way to help your performance. If you eat nourishing food early in the day, you're less likely to feel hungry enough to eat high-fat snacks like ice cream and doughnuts later in the day.

If there's no time to cook, choose an iron-enriched, low-sugar cold cereal and top it with a sliced banana or raisins and low-fat milk or yogurt for a quick breakfast that won't make you feel bloated.

Some teenagers involved in athletics take enormous amounts of individual vitamins without knowing anything about them except what a salesperson tells them. Vitamins and minerals are necessary for good health. But why they work is still a mystery—even to scientists. Much of the research being done now stresses the interactions among vitamins and minerals—that is, how each influences the others. Because the body is so finely tuned, it may be easy to upset the balance between vitamins and minerals by taking a large amount of any single one.

It's reasonable to take one standard multivitamin supplement with minerals each day. And, if you want, take an extra 500 to 1,000 milligrams of vitamin C each day. Vitamin C plays an important role in wound healing. But remember, vitamin and mineral supplements are just that—supplements—not substitutes for a good diet.

Teenage girls in particular don't get enough iron or calcium from their diets. Speak to your doctor about supplementing these minerals. If you're tired all the time, or catch every cold or sore throat that's going around, or if you have prolonged or irregular menstrual periods, you may be anemic.

CHAPTER 4

Warming Up and Cooling Down

We call sports "games" because they're fun to play—and it's tempting to get out on the field or court and start playing as soon as possible. But any sports activity demands vigorous, high performance from your body. Just as you can't expect a car to get from 0 to 60 miles per hour in nothing flat—or stop without first slowing down—you can't expect your body to go from resting to peak performance in nothing flat—or stop without slowing down—without the risk of some harm.

Warm-up, Cool-down, and Stretching

WARMING UP Beginning a workout without warming up is like trying a high dive without knowing how to swim. Sooner or later your luck will run out and you'll get hurt.

Why is it so important to warm up?

When you exercise, your muscles contract and get

29

shorter. Short, tight muscles strain and tear more easily than loose, flexible muscles. Warm-ups prepare your body for exercise and bring it from an inactive state to a state of readiness for strenuous activity. They warm your muscles and tendons, increase the blood flow to muscles, increase your heart and pulse rate, and raise your internal temperature to its ideal level for peak performance.

You're less likely to injure your muscles if you warm up because the increase of blood supply to the muscles raises their temperature, making them pliable and permitting them to stretch. Pliable, elastic muscles also respond more quickly to sudden movement, which helps to prevent injury.

Warming up properly helps you perform better in other ways, as well. Your response time is faster because nerve messages travel faster. Muscle contractions are faster and more powerful. And, if you warm up, your performance time can improve by as much as 6 percent in a speed event of 100 meters to 800 meters. Warming up also improves flexibility, which enables your body to endure the physical stress of sports and prevent injuries. Also, flexible joints have more range of motion than inflexible ones—and a greater range of motion is directly tied to improved performance.

How long should you warm up?

Fifteen minutes of warm-up will improve your performance more than five minutes of warm-up. Any longer than that certainly won't hurt, but it won't help particularly. If you have the time, warming up properly is a good investment in playing well. If you join an informal game on the spur of the moment, you probably won't want to take the time. But spend at least a few minutes warming up if you can.

A good warm-up includes four steps.

Step 1 loosens major joints. Take approximately one minute to rotate your neck, make large arm circles, bend at the waist, bring your knees to your chest, and rotate your ankles.

Step 2, general warm-up, involves light to moderate exercise. Spend between two and five minutes on general exercise that includes actively moving all your major muscle groups—your arms, trunk, back, hips, and legs. Light jogging, calisthenics, or jumping rope all work well. Exercise until you break into a light sweat, but not so strenuously that you get too tired to go on.

Step 3 focuses on flexibility. Flexible muscles work better, so spend between eight and ten minutes stretching out. The purpose of these exercises is to pull your muscles to full extension slowly. You do this in two stages, sometimes called "first pull" or "easy stretch" and "second pull" or "developmental stretch." Stretch each muscle gradually—until you can feel tension, but not pain (first pull position). Hold the stretch for ten to thirty seconds; the feeling of tension will ease. Then move slightly further than the easy stretch (second pull position). Hold this stretch for ten to thirty seconds. Relax. Repeat the stretch three times. Easy does it— don't stretch until it hurts. "No pain, no gain" doesn't

31

apply to stretching. In fact, if it hurts, you're doing something wrong.

Don't bounce when you stretch. Some athletes used to bounce when they stretched out their muscles—exercises called "ballistic stretching." But these rapid, jerking, bouncing movements work against you, rather than for you. When you stretch using fast, jerky, bouncy movements, your muscle contracts, rather than relaxes, to protect itself from overstretching. This actually shortens the muscle and prevents you from stretching it fully. Bouncing can also cause painful tears in muscle fiber, which scar over and leave the muscles even less flexible.

There are times when stretching may hurt rather than help. Stretching a cold muscle can injure it, so don't stretch until you've already warmed your muscles by going through Step 1 and Step 2. Also, don't be tempted to stretch if you've torn a muscle or a tendon. In order to heal properly, injured muscles and tendons need rest—not stretching. After it feels better—anywhere from two days to a couple of weeks—you may begin stretching.

Step 4 of a warm-up is sport specific. At this stage, you begin practicing the kinds of skills involved in the sport you're about to play. If you're a basketball player, for instance, you can shoot baskets; if you're playing baseball, exercise by throwing a ball. Football players can practice offensive and defensive plays, soccer players can dribble a ball at an easy pace. Whatever your sport or activity, spend five minutes (or longer if you'd like) practicing your technique. This kind of realistic practice makes warming up more interesting.

Once you've warmed up, don't wait more than fifteen minutes before starting practice or a game. Some coaches now encourage their teams to warm up during halftime as well.

COOLING DOWN Cooling down is as important for your body as warming up. You may be tempted to skip a cool-down and rush out the gym door or off the field once you've finished playing. Don't. Bodies don't automatically repair themselves after strenuous exercise. During exercise, muscle contractions signal the body to widen veins and arteries. Your heart pumps faster and your blood pressure rises. Blood is diverted from the rest of the body to deliver much-needed oxygen to your heart and other muscles. When you stop exercising, your muscles stop contracting; less blood is pumped back to the heart, and blood tends to pool in your arms and legs. Because of this, less oxygen is available to the rest of your body, and you might feel light-headed or dizzy.

Cool-downs allow your body to return to its resting state gradually. Your muscles are tight after a workout, and the muscle cells need a supply of fresh oxygen. Waste products that build up during exercise, such as excess lactic acid, can cause fatigue if they're not removed. Keeping your body in motion and stretching your muscles after a workout keeps the blood flowing—delivering oxygen to your muscles. If you include some stretching exercises at the end of your cool-down, you can lessen the muscle soreness that often results from a workout.

Cooling down can be as simple as walking briskly or jogging until your breathing returns to normal, and then stretching the muscles you used most during your exercise or workout—thigh muscles for cyclists, hamstrings for runners and tennis players, all major muscle groups for weight lifters. Ease gradually into the stretch, breathe deeply, and bend slowly. Spend at least ten to fifteen minutes on a cool-down, including stretching exercises.

CHAPTER 5

Stretching

Stretching helps protect against injury by developing flexible and supple muscles. In addition, if you have been injured, easy stretching can help you get your muscles back into shape while the injury heals.

Here are some basic rules to keep in mind:

Never force cold muscles to stretch. Start stretching only after you warm up with two to five minutes of light jogging, jumping rope, or calisthenics. Hold each stretch for ten to thirty seconds—without bouncing. Although your muscles will feel tense when you start, the feeling of tension will ease. At that point, stretch a little further and hold it for ten to thirty seconds. Repeat each stretch three times.

Remember to breathe. Don't give in to the temptation to hold your breath while you stretch. Breathe slowly and rhythmically during stretching.

Some typical stretching exercises are listed below.

Don't feel you have to do every one of them every day. Start with a few exercises and add new ones or substitute others as you become more flexible.

General Stretching to Start Out

1. While standing, look over your right shoulder, turning your head as far as you can. Hold for ten seconds. Then look over your left shoulder. Hold for ten seconds.

2. Raise your shoulders to your ears as high as you can. Hold for five seconds. Relax them slowly.

3. Clasp your hands above your head, palms facing toward the ceiling. Push your arms up as far as you can reach. Hold this stretch for fifteen seconds. Relax slowly.

4. Raise your arms and drop them behind your head. Grasp the elbow of one arm with the hand of the other arm. Pull the elbow gently and slowly. Hold the stretch for fifteen seconds. Stretch the other arm in the same way.

5. Stand with your feet comfortably apart and your knees bent slightly. Hold your arms over your head and bend from the hips to your right side. Hold the stretch for ten seconds and then bend to your left side.

6. Stand with your legs spread about 18 inches apart, knees slightly bent, hands on your waist. Slowly and smoothly turn to the right, come back to starting position, and turn to the left.

7. Lie down on your back on a mat or on the floor. Bend your knees and let them drop toward the floor, placing the soles of your feet together. Hold this position for thirty seconds. Don't push your knees toward the floor—let gravity pull them.

8. Still lying on your back on a mat or the floor, pull one leg toward your chest holding your knee with both hands. Hold for thirty seconds. Repeat with the other leg.

Upper-Body Stretching

SHOULDERS 1. Holding your hands over your shoulders, elbows bent, grasp a small towel. Pull on the towel, straighten your arms behind you and raise them as far as you can. Hold for ten seconds and lower your arms slowly and smoothly.

2. Hold one end of a towel with your left hand and drop the other end over your left shoulder. Grab the towel with your right hand by reaching up behind your waist. Pull down on the towel with your right hand, stretching your left shoulder gently. Change sides.

3. Hold your arms straight in front of you, hands together, fingers laced. Turn your palms away from your body and push outward. Hold for fifteen seconds, then relax.

BACK 1. Kneel down on the floor or on a mat. Stretch your arms straight in front of you; place the palms of your hands flat on the ground. Pull up with straight arms without moving your hands. Hold the pull for fifteen seconds, then relax.

2. Kneel on your hands and knees. Lower your head and exhale. Gently arch your back, pushing the small of your back toward the ceiling, like a cat stretching. Hold for five seconds. Inhale and come back to starting position slowly. Raise your head and exhale again. Gently arch your back in the opposite direction by pushing the small of your back toward the floor. Hold for five seconds. Inhale and return to starting position.

3. Lying on your back on the floor or on a mat, hold your arms out over your head and point your toes. Pull your arms and legs in the opposite direction. Hold for five seconds and relax.

Lower-Body Stretching

HIPS To stretch the hips, lower back, and hamstrings, stand with your knees bent slightly, and your feet about 18 inches apart and pointed straight ahead. Drop your head, bend at the waist, and let your arms dangle loosely. Hold for twenty seconds. To take the strain off your lower back, remember to keep your knees bent any time

40

you bend at the waist to stretch. Next, keeping your knees bent, gently push yourself upright, using the muscles of your upper leg.

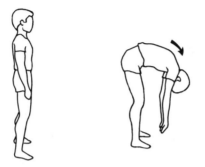

HAMSTRINGS AND QUADRICEPS The hamstrings, muscles that run down the back of your leg from the pelvic bone to below the knee, enable you to bend your knees and straighten your hips. The quadriceps, muscles that run along the front of your leg from the pelvic bone to below the knee, extend the knee and flex the hips. Because these two groups of muscles have opposing actions, tightening one group will relax the other.

HAMSTRINGS 1. Sit down on the floor and rest your back against a wall. Stretch your left leg straight in front of you. Bend your right knee, grasp the outside of your ankle with your left hand, and put your right hand and forearm around your left knee. Pull your right leg toward your chest until you feel a gentle stretch in your hamstring. Hold for thirty seconds. Change sides.

41

2. Stand up and cross your ankles, right over left. Bend down and hold the backs of your ankles with your hands. Pull your upper body to your thighs. Hold the stretch for thirty seconds.

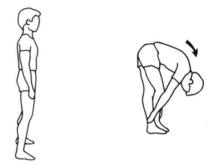

QUADRICEPS   1. Lie face down on the floor or on a mat. Reach back and grab your right ankle with your left hand. Gently pull your foot down to your buttocks. Hold for thirty seconds. Release and repeat with your left ankle and right hand.

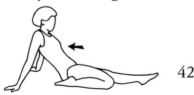

2. Sit down on the floor or on a mat with your feet in front of you. Bend your right leg so that your right heel is next to your right hip. Keep your left leg straight. Lean back slowly, using your arms for support, until you feel a stretch. Hold for twenty seconds and release. Repeat with your left leg.

CALF   1. Stand about 12 inches away from a wall. Bend your arms and rest your forearms on the wall. Keep your feet flat on the floor and pointed straight ahead. Bend your right knee and put your left leg straight behind you. Slowly lean forward against the wall. Hold for twenty seconds. Alternate leg positions and repeat.

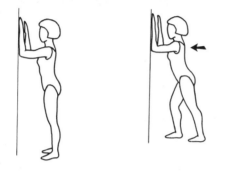

2. Stand about 24 inches away from a wall. With your arms straight out, place the palms of your hands flat on the wall. Keeping your knees straight, bend your arms and lean against the wall with your chest. Hold for twenty seconds, then push yourself back to starting position.

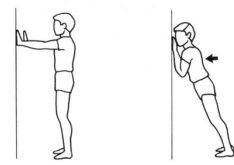

CHAPTER 6

The Psychological Side of Sports

It isn't enough to be in top physical condition. To perform at your best, you need to be fit emotionally as well. Your mind and your emotions play an essential role in any sports activity.

An athlete who isn't physically fit complains of being out of shape, but an athlete who's lost the emotional edge to play a winning game complains of a slump or, worse, of burnout. Generally speaking, there are three ingredients that make a difference in being emotionally prepared to play: concentration, commitment, and spirit. Burnout can result from the loss of any one of these three.

CONCENTRATION may be as simple as keeping your eye on the ball. But even that is not as easy as it sounds. A cheering crowd—or a jeering one—or the sudden sight of an airplane, or a friend calling out your name, can easily distract you. And that moment's distraction can cause you to miss the shot.

In team sports it's even more complicated. While concentrating on your own position and task, you have to watch both your teammates and your opponents, be aware of their moves, and think a step or two ahead.

Sometimes emotional problems that have nothing at all to do with sports can affect your performance. If you're worried about your grades or problems with your parents or illness in the family, you're not going to be able to concentrate fully on your athletic performance.

When athletes burn out, they just can't keep their mind on the game. They go through the motions, make the right moves, look alert—all without paying full attention. Their thoughts wander off to other concerns. They think of something the coach said, of how last night's practice session wasn't as good as they hoped, of an upcoming game next week. They recall an argument with a friend or spot a buddy in the stands. But even if they're diverted only momentarily, their performance suffers.

COMMITMENT also plays a role in sports. Everyone wants to be the star player on the team, and it would be nice to be able to fill that role just by wishing. But it doesn't work that way. Ace players or performers get there only after long hours of practice. Sometimes it means getting up in the morning to practice while everyone else is asleep. Sometimes it means giving up a movie with friends. But whatever it means and whatever else top athletes have to give up or do without, what motivates them is a commitment to being the best at what they're doing.

Suddenly it all seems to be too much, although everything's been going well. You've been improving steadily in practice, the coach depends on you, and your parents boast about what an asset you are to the team. But the unending practices, competitions, and road trips start to lose their shine. Sometimes it creeps up on you. Sometimes it happens overnight. You find yourself tired for no reason, your performance is off, your muscles hurt, you can't even think straight, and you feel sick from headaches or stomachaches. Practice is a bore, competitions don't mean anything, and you feel that it makes absolutely no difference whether or not you continue in your sport. You've lost your energy and you've lost your enthusiasm. But most basic of all, you've lost your commitment. You're burned out.

SPIRIT Some people call it nerve, still others call it heart. But whatever you call it, it's another emotion that contributes to success in sports. Spirit is the willingness to take risks, the readiness to go all-out to win, the enthusiasm that enables you to push on in spite of the weather, or fatigue, or the number of hours you've already put in.

Everyone knows about team spirit—and every athlete knows that it deserts you at times. You've heard athletes say, "The team's been in a slump lately." But individual athletes also lose heart. They say, "It wasn't one of my days," or "I was just off today."

46

Loss of spirit can affect you in another way as well: You find yourself getting hurt more often during practice or competition, and minor injuries bother you more than they used to. Without quite knowing how it happens, you've begun to think that an injury is an acceptable alternative to the pressures of competition or the rigors of practice. After all, an injured athlete isn't the same as one who quits. You won't lose face if you can't play because you've been injured.

So you exaggerate minor injuries or convince yourself that a bruise or a strain still hurts many weeks later, even though the team trainer or your doctor can't find anything wrong. That points to burnout.

You may also find yourself getting hurt if you're on a team only because you want to impress your classmates or because you're trying to please your parents, because the coach thinks you're built for a certain sport, or because your friends think you're great at it—and not because you really enjoy it. Athletes get hurt more readily and more frequently if the motive for participating is anything but love of the sport.

The trouble is that even if you begin because you love the sport, the better you are, the more is asked of you. Once you begin to compete outside the neighborhood and make the varsity team or go on to statewide meets, the pressure of competition and discipline begins to build up the level of stress.

Some athletes can withstand the pressure and even thrive on it. Others don't know how to deal with the stresses of athletic competition—and they burn out.

They begin to find competition threatening rather than exciting; they worry that they'll fail their teammates and be viewed negatively by them. Burnout develops when you perceive the emotional demands and pressures of participating in a sport as greater than your ability to cope with them. It's the product of unremitting stress. You lose your enthusiasm and energy to participate in sports. It's just not fun anymore. The satisfaction of honing your skills during practice has turned to sheer drudgery. The demands are too great, and the only way to cope is to escape from the pressures.

Stress isn't the only cause of burnout, however. These symptoms of burnout may reflect an undetected physical problem that shows up as loss of energy or enthusiasm. So if sports seem to be growing stale and participating isn't fun any longer, the first thing to do is see your doctor for a physical checkup. You may not be able to give it your all because you're anemic. Or you may have gained or lost too much weight too quickly—and that can affect your ability to exercise.

You *can* do something about burnout. If your doctor gives you a clean bill of health, speak to your coach about changing your routine or cutting down on practice time for a while. Sometimes these simple changes are enough. Take time to balance the demands of athletic achievement with other activities. Although you're sure you don't have the time to go to the movies with friends or take a walk or run an errand for a neighbor, give yourself a break. The time away from sports and the emotional lift of another activity may be enough to renew your energy and motivation—and, consequently, your performance. If that doesn't work, you need to look at your motive for participating and ask yourself why your sport isn't any fun anymore.

Winning and Losing

You first started in your sport because participating was fun. Often that sense of fun gets lost because the need to win becomes the most important aspect of participating. Yet every athlete knows that if you get too preoccupied with winning—or with losing—that alone can make you choke.

In any sport or game, when someone wins, someone also loses. No one likes to lose, but losing a close game doesn't mean you've failed. You may feel like a failure if you're playing just to please the crowd or your parents or the coach. Pressure from any of these outside sources may make you feel that the only point of playing is to win.

Really good athletes only get bored if they always win. They begin to look for tougher competition. By the same token athletes who play against competition that always outranks them soon lose interest. For sports to have any meaning, you have to find the level of competition you enjoy.

If the only thing that matters is winning, then the sport itself doesn't matter. And anyone who asks you to play only to win is treating you unfairly. If your whole worth as a person depends on winning, every game or meet or tournament can threaten your very being. And no one can bear up under that kind of pressure for long—it will eventually destroy your entire sense of yourself.

Mental Preparation

Having a positive image of yourself as a competitor is crucial in sports—as in anything else. After all, how can you do your best when you think everyone else out there can beat you? There are some simple ways to develop your self-image. Whenever you find yourself thinking that you don't have the ability or the skills to compete against others, think of the races you've won or of the times your team walked away with the victory.

Setting unreasonable expectations for yourself may cause you to tense up so much that you actually perform below par. If you find yourself choking up or overcompensating or missing shots that should be a snap because you're so focused on winning, try setting a goal that has to do not with victory but with how well you'll perform that day. Think about the time you want to make in the sprint, rather than finishing first. Think about perfecting your form in the backstroke, rather than beating the swimmer in the next lane.

It may help to keep a training log to keep track of the times you feel negative about yourself. When does it happen? How long do they last? Then make a list of the things that make you feel good about yourself. Where do the two lists differ? What changes can you make in your schedule or training so that you'll be in more situations where you feel good about yourself?

Imagery

Have you ever awakened from a nightmare with your heart thumping and your pajamas soaked with perspiration? The nightmare wasn't real, it was "just a dream," and yet you reacted to it physically just as if the frightening events were actually happening. Researchers know that the body responds physically to imaginary thoughts or perceptions and that mental images, and the emotions they evoke, directly affect performance. In other words, in some ways the body can't tell the difference between a real situation and an imaginary one.

You can use the power of imagery—mental pictures of an event—to improve your performance and increase your confidence. Using imagery, you can "practice" your performance before an upcoming event in order to overcome obstacles you think you may encounter or to "see" yourself winning. You can practice your best moves—or swings—or dives—even if you've got a charley horse or a sprained ankle. You can mentally rehearse every second of a competition in advance of the actual event to provide that slight emotional lift that may make the difference between first and second place.

Before a game or a meet, try to imagine the event in detail. Close your eyes, and watch yourself rehearse your performance and plan your strategy in your mind. Conduct your rehearsal in "real time," just as though it were really happening. Listen for the starter's gun, hear the crowd cheering, feel the heat of the sun, smell the grass, picture your competition. Concentrate on a vivid image of how you will perform correctly and successfully. If you've had trouble with a specific movement, picture yourself doing it correctly every time. If you're competing in an individual sport, picture the time you set as a goal posted at the end of the event. Repeat your mental rehearsal many times before a competition. Of course, mental imagery alone won't help you win. But combined with practice, imagining yourself doing well can help make it happen.

CHAPTER 7

Common
Physical Problems

Although most of the injuries and physical problems that arise from athletics may seem terrible while you're suffering from them or if you're sidelined during an important game, many of them are relatively minor. You may be able to ease the pain and discomfort easily.

Some, like athlete's foot and jock itch, are merely annoying—skin conditions that affect athletes and nonathletes alike. Athlete's foot and jock itch may look frightening, but they're not dangerous. Both infections are usually caused by a tiny, plantlike microorganism called a fungus.

ATHLETE'S FOOT (tinea pedis) usually begins in the space between the third and fourth toes and then spreads to the soles of the feet. The infection causes redness, and cracking and peeling skin between the toes. Sometimes the infected area burns and becomes sensitive to touch. In hot weather, the rash may flare up and become painful.

You're either susceptible to athlete's foot or you're not. If you are, you're more likely to develop athlete's foot if you spend a lot of time in sweaty socks and sneakers; the fungus that causes it thrives in warm, moist places.

A lot of commonly used remedies *won't* prevent athlete's foot. Boiling your socks, treating your shoes, or using antifungal foot baths are of little value. The only way to *prevent* athlete's foot is to keep your feet dry.

Dry your feet well after showering or bathing, especially between the toes and under them. Then dust your feet with either plain talcum powder or an antifungal powder. Also sprinkle the powder inside your shoes or sneakers. Wear dry, absorbent cotton or wool socks and change them at least once a day.

If you do develop athlete's foot, make sure to keep your feet as dry as possible. Use cotton or wool socks and change into a clean pair several times a day. Powder your feet every time you change your socks. Avoid using ointments, which trap moisture. If possible, wear sandals or walk around barefoot several times a day. If the infection doesn't start to clear up in a week or two, see your doctor.

JOCK ITCH (tinea cruris), a close relative of athlete's foot, is the common term for an infection affecting the groin. Jock itch isn't limited to "jocks"—or even to boys, although boys who are physically active and perspire heavily are most likely to be affected.

Jock itch, a burning, painful, itchy rash, is usually caused by a fungus—but it can also be caused by bacteria, or, sometimes, a combination of both. The rash can be caused by the same fungus that causes athlete's foot—the infection spreads from the feet to the groin. Jock itch can also be caused by underpants or a jockstrap that chafes or irritates the body. If the rash appeared just after you started wearing new underpants or a new jockstrap, that may be the cause. Again, it's not that serious, but it can be embarrassing and sufficiently painful to interfere with your concentration and performance.

If you develop jock itch, switch to loose cotton underwear. Nylon and polyester tend to trap moisture. Never reuse underwear or jockstraps without washing them first. Dry your skin carefully after you shower or bathe, and use talcum powder to keep the area dry. As with athlete's foot, if the rash doesn't start to clear up in a week or two, see your doctor.

BLISTERS develop when skin is rubbed repeatedly and the top layer becomes separated from the lower layer. Fluid accumulates between the layers, causing the liquid-filled swelling. Blisters usually develop on the hands or feet.

If you do get a blister and it doesn't hurt, cover it over with a Band-Aid and leave it alone. If it does hurt, you can open it to relieve the pressure. First, wash off the skin with soap and water, then pierce the side of the blister— not the top—with a sterilized needle and gently squeeze out the fluid. (To sterilize a needle, hold it in the flame of a match for two or three seconds.) Dab the blister with an antiseptic and cover it with a Band-Aid or tape a gauze pad over it. Don't break a blister by peeling away the top layer of skin. This leaves the lower layer unprotected and slows healing. If the area around the blister becomes red and feels hot, or if it starts to ooze pus, the blister is infected. See a doctor.

Of course, it's much better to avoid blisters in the first place. You can do that by breaking in new athletic shoes or equipment gradually. Wear new shoes around the house for an hour on the first day, then increase the time an hour each day for three or four days. Also make sure that your socks don't bunch up in your shoes. Wrinkled socks will rub the skin of your feet and probably cause blisters. There's another trick you can try. Wear two pairs of socks together. Put on the first pair inside out and wear the second pair right side out on top of the first pair. The socks will rub against each other—but not against your feet.

A STITCH is a sharp, sudden pain in your abdomen near the lower rib cage. A stitch is a form of muscle cramp. Usually the pain is on the right side and feels sharper when you inhale. Stitches may have several different causes, including being out of shape, overeating, exercising too soon after eating, eating "gassy" foods such as broccoli or beans, or drinking carbonated soda before exercising. A stitch is irritating, but it won't injure you.

If you tend to get stitches when you run, slow your pace to see if that helps. If it doesn't, there are several things you can do to ease a stitch. Try one or more of the following remedies:

1. Take a deep breath and blow it out through pursed lips.

2. If the stitch is on your right side, stretch your right arm over your head as high as you can. If it's on your left side, stretch your left arm over your head.

3. Lie down on your back and raise both arms over your head. The stitch should ease up after a few moments.

When you work a muscle too hard, or stretch it too much or too suddenly, it can go into a prolonged, painful contraction called a SPASM. A local muscle spasm is called a cramp.

Stretching a cramped muscle is the best way to relieve it. To relieve a calf cramp, for instance, pull your foot up gently. To relieve a cramp in your arm, raise your arm over your head as high as it will go. Once the muscle begins to relax, massage it gently.

If you spent your summer lying around the beach, or didn't do anything more strenuous than walk from the refrigerator to the back porch, you'll probably complain of sore muscles when you first start sports training in the fall. The pain is temporary, and generally lasts only a day or two. Relax in a warm-water bath after your first training session or two—and make sure you warm up, stretch, and cool down properly.

Lame horses are nicknamed "Charley." If your thigh muscles are bruised by a kick, a fall, or a sharp blow, the torn muscle fibers can become tender, painful, and perhaps swollen, depending on the severity of the bruise. This injury is called a CHARLEY HORSE. If the bruise is minor, you won't feel any pain or muscle tightness for several hours. If it's more severe, pain and muscle spasms develop immediately, but you can still move your knee normally. If you've got a really severe bruise, your thigh will swell up and you won't be able to move your knee normally.

Treat charley horses with RICE.

RICE

The trouble with minor injuries is that if you don't treat them, they're likely to become major injuries. No practice, game, competition, or meet is worth that price.

When you're bruised, small blood vessels break and leak blood into surrounding tissues. Within half an hour the tissues start to swell, and this swelling can cause more damage than the injury itself. You can limit swelling with RICE, an acronym for *r*est, *i*ce, *c*ompression, and *e*levation.

1. Rest. Stop exercising. If you don't, you force more blood into the damaged tissue. Rest until the damaged area stops hurting, then begin normal activity cautiously. Depending on the extent of the injury, you may have to rest for a few minutes—or a few days. Usually, you only have to rest the injured part. If your wrist is injured, you can still run. If your foot is injured, you may still be able to use free weights.

2. Ice. Ice deadens pain, reduces bleeding by causing

blood vessels to contract, and helps to reduce swelling and inflammation. Apply an ice pack, ice in a plastic bag, or an ice cup to the injured area. Never apply ice directly to your skin—wrap the pack, bag, or cup in a towel or cloth first. During the first hour after the injury, keep the ice pack on for ten to twenty minutes and then take if off for twenty minutes. Then apply it for twenty minutes and take it off for an hour. Repeat this several times for the first two days after an injury.

3. Compression. For most minor injuries you don't have to do more than wrap an elastic bandage around the injured area. Compression helps to reduce swelling by preventing the accumulation of fluid. If the area hurts or feels numb when you apply the bandage, loosen it a bit. The bandage should be snug but not tight.

4. Elevation. Elevate the injured area higher than your heart so gravity will drain excess fluid from it. You don't have to elevate it much. It's enough to rest your arm or leg on a couple of pillows when you're lying down.

CHAPTER 8

Lower-Body Injuries

To understand how to avoid injuries that will take you out of play, you need to know what can go wrong. This chapter on lower-body injuries and the next on upper-body injuries describe the most common sports injuries and what to do about them. However, the first-aid measures described in these two chapters are no substitute for medical attention. Since an unattended injury may knock you out of competition for the rest of the season, it's important to be open with your coach about your injuries and to make sure you get sufficient medical attention. Don't try to tough it out. You risk turning a slight injury into something far more serious.

Except for the trapeze, flying rings, and parallel bars, everything starts from the ground up—and healthy feet and legs are of key importance to participating in sports activities.

Feet and Ankles

Foot injuries are sometimes annoying and nothing more. Other times they can force you off the field or out of competition. Most of the time, injuries to your feet and legs hurt a lot, but they're not dangerous.

TOES Your toes come in for more than their fair share of injuries. They get stepped on, stubbed, kicked, and jammed into the ends of your sneakers or shoes. Small wonder they're so readily injured.

BRUISED TOES. A sudden blow to your foot can cause bleeding under the toenail (or to your fingernail if you bruise your finger). If you stub your toe or someone steps on it, you may notice either immediately or within a couple of hours that the nail looks red and the toe hurts. In a day or two, the nail turns black.

Blood trapped under the nail causes the pain. If the pain is really severe, your doctor can drain the trapped blood. If it doesn't bother you too much, leave the nail alone. It will fall off in two or three weeks and a new nail will form in its place.

SPRAINED TOES. If you've ever walked barefoot and caught your small toe on the edge of a bureau or chair, you know how much it hurts. Sprained toes often result from just this kind of accident. If you do sprain your toe, the base of the toe will swell up quickly and the toe will feel painful when you move it.

The best way to ease the pain of a sprained toe is to

keep off your feet as much as possible and apply ice for a few days. (See RICE, Chapter 7, page 58.)

BROKEN TOES. Sometimes the force of catching your toe or banging it is severe enough to break the bone. Broken toes generally swell up immediately and hurt. A broken toe may also look oddly deformed.

Only very severe breaks require casts. Otherwise, the broken toe is taped firmly to the one next to it until the bone heals, generally about two to four weeks.

TURF TOE. Football, baseball, or soccer players face the problem of "turf toe," caused by suddenly jamming the big toe forward. You may find that you jam your toe once, but then you go back to playing because it feels better. Then it happens again. But this time, your toe becomes tender, red, stiff, and swollen.

Early treatment for turf toe includes icing, a compression dressing, and elevating the affected foot (RICE). Two or three days after it happens, your doctor will likely tape your toe to prevent moving it too much. You can probably start playing again when the swelling goes down and the toe stops hurting.

You're more likely to develop turf toe if you wear soft-soled shoes or the wrong type of shoe for the sport or the surface you're playing on. Shoes designed for natural turf have long, pointed cleats. Shoes designed for artificial turf have more but shorter cleats.

HEELS

HEEL BRUISES. Heel bruises generally affect jumpers, hurdlers, and basketball players because they're most likely to land hard on their heels. But you can also get a heel bruise from wearing cleats, from exercising in thin-soled shoes, or from running on rocks or other hard surfaces.

Although they're not serious, heel bruises are painful. When you bruise your heel, the tissue between the skin of the heel and the periosteum, the tough, fibrous membrane that covers the heelbone, becomes swollen. You can relieve the pain of a heel bruise by keeping an ice bag on it for fifteen minutes to half an hour after it first happens. Use foam rubber inserts or heel pads in both your athletic shoes and street shoes until you don't feel any more pain. Heel bruises take anywhere from ten days to three weeks to heal completely.

You can prevent heel bruises by using heel cups, pads, or foam rubber inserts in your shoes to lessen the shock to your heels.

HEEL SPURS. Heel spurs are small, bumpy outgrowths of bone under the heel. In some instances heel spurs cause no pain at all; in other instances heel spurs make you feel as if you're walking on pebbles.

Special arch supports, heel cups, or pads can relieve the pain associated with heel spurs. Rarely, you may have to have the spurs removed surgically.

PLANTAR FASCIITIS. The plantar fascia ("plantar" means bottom; "fascia" is a tough, fibrous material) is a protective band of tissue that runs along the bottom of your foot from your heelbone to the base of your toes. The plantar fascia supports the arch of your foot and keeps it from collapsing under pressure.

When you run or walk, the plantar fascia stretches as your body's weight spreads your foot. But the tissue isn't elastic, and can't stretch out and spring back to shape, so with repeated stress and overuse, something gives. Small tears develop and the tissue becomes inflamed. The plantar fascia may also pull away slightly from the heelbone. Sometimes bone spurs develop. Walking and running further damage the tissue and aggravate the problem.

When the tissue becomes inflamed, the condition is called plantar fasciitis (the suffix "-itis" means inflamed), or heel spur syndrome. Plantar fasciitis most often affects endurance athletes such as cross-country and track runners.

The most painful symptom occurs in the morning, when you first step down on your foot. Sometimes the pain is so severe that you have to walk on your toes for a few steps. Pain increases after walking and running, and may be severe enough to radiate up the back of the leg. Your heel may also swell up.

Apply ice to reduce the swelling and inflammation, and take ibuprofen (Advil or Medipren, for instance). Doctors do not recommend aspirin routinely because in some rare cases, for unknown reasons, an adolescent who takes aspirin when certain viral diseases are present runs a small risk of developing a severe inflammation of the liver and brain called Reye's syndrome. Most important, restrict any weight-bearing activities for the first day or two and then start again slowly. Using arch supports in both shoes will reduce stretching the plantar fascia and allow it to heal. Also use sponge-rubber heel pads, a heel cup, or doughnut-shaped cutout padding. Apply ice after workouts and before bed until the pain goes away.

To prevent plantar fasciitis from developing in the first place, wear shoes that have flexible soles, adequate padding in the heel, and good arch support. You may also want to tape or strap your foot before an athletic event.

ANKLES

ANKLE SPRAIN. A sprain is an injury to a ligament, the connection between two bones. The most common type of ankle sprain occurs on the side, when you suddenly turn your foot inward. Never continue to play or run on a sprained ankle. Use ice, compression, and elevation immediately.

Ankle sprains are classified according to their severity. In a mild (Grade 1) sprain you'll notice mild pain and some swelling. Treat your ankle with ice and a compression or elastic bandage and high-top shoes for a day or two. A moderate (Grade 2) sprain is one in which the ligament is actually torn, so walking or putting any weight on your foot really hurts. In addition to ice, compression, and elevation, your doctor might want you to use crutches for two or three days and then start gentle exercises. A Grade 2 sprain takes two or three weeks to heal completely. The pain and swelling are so severe in a Grade 3 sprain that you can't put any weight on your foot at all or move your ankle. Your doctor may put your foot in a cast and have you use crutches for anywhere from two weeks to a month. After the cast is removed, you'll go through a series of rehabilitation exercises.

FRACTURED ANKLES. A fracture is a break in a bone. Ankle fractures can range from a slight chip to several broken bones. Small fractures cause mild swelling and pain. More severe fractures cause considerable pain and swelling.

Don't try to diagnose your own ankle injury. Only a professional can distinguish between a severe sprain and a fracture—and often only with an X ray.

Legs and Knees

LEGS

SHIN SPLINTS. The term "shin splint" refers to a throbbing pain along the lower leg, especially along the shin. Sometimes the calf of the leg is tender and the calf muscles are tight. The scientific name for shin splints is medial tibial syndrome; the tibia is the main bone in the lower leg.

No one is quite sure just why shin splints develop. One theory attributes them to excessive training, which leads to soft tissue inflammation. Another theory suggests that shin splints result from an inflammation of the tough, fibrous membrane that covers the tibia and attaches it to the muscle. Still others attribute shin splints to microfractures of the bone or inflammation of the muscle. Most likely, shin splints are caused by a combination of these factors.

Shin splints are especially common in runners, and often related to jumping on a hard surface, running on the front of the foot, running on concrete or other hard surfaces, or wearing the wrong kind of shoes. Generally, shin splints hurt along the shin, and the area is tender to the touch. The pain usually starts after athletic activity and continues until you start your next workout. The pain disappears while you're active, but then starts again when you finish working out. If you don't do anything about them, the pain and tenderness become worse and eventually affect your performance.

The best thing for shin splints is rest; the earlier you stop your activity and give your legs a chance to heal, the faster your legs will mend. The first stage of treating shin splints is to apply ice packs to the sore area three or four times a day for five to fifteen minutes. Always follow the ice packs with gentle stretching. After three or four weeks, you can probably start jogging for short distances. At this point, use ice packs twice a day, before and after physical activity.

If you're a runner, you may be able to avoid a recurrence by wearing running shoes with cushioned heels and soles, using orthotics (contoured foot supports), and running or jogging only on a soft track or grass. Also, be sure you warm up properly before every workout.

If you suffer from shin splints that don't feel better in two or three weeks, see a doctor to make sure you haven't developed a stress fracture.

STRESS FRACTURE. Runners are particularly susceptible to hairline cracks, called stress fractures, which usually occur in the bones of the feet and legs. Stress fractures, generally caused by overuse, may not be visible on an X ray for several weeks after they occur. A stress fracture can be extremely painful, especially when touched, and the pain becomes more acute with walking and running.

Because the bone is cracked, not broken, you probably won't need a cast. But do only flex and stretch exercises until the bone is healed and you don't feel any more pain. If you've had one stress fracture, you may be prone to a recurrence. To decrease the chances of it happening again, wear well-cushioned shoes, don't overdo it, and run on soft surfaces.

TENDINITIS. Tendons are bands of connective tissue that join muscles to bones. Tendinitis—an inflamed, painful, swollen tendon—usually results from overuse or from pressure on a tendon. If you're a runner, you may be hit with Achilles tendinitis, an inflammation of the heel cord (Achilles tendon), which joins the two major muscles at the back of the leg to the back of the heelbone.

The inflamed tendon hurts when you start exercising, but may feel better once you've warmed up. The pain comes back a few hours after you stop exercising. You can relieve the pain of tendinitis with ice and an anti-inflammatory medication such as ibuprofen. After the pain disappears, start stretching exercises for the Achilles tendon. Standing at arm's length from a wall, lean against it and slowly bend your elbows while your heels remain on the floor. Hold the stretch for ten seconds and then push yourself away from the wall. Do these push-aways before and after every workout. To prevent tendinitis, take the time for a proper warm-up before you start exercising, and stretch out after exercise.

MUSCLE PULLS. A muscle pull is another name for a muscle strain—an injury to muscle fibers. Warming up improperly or for too short a time can cause pulled muscles.

If you do pull a muscle, stop exercising and put an ice pack on the injured area as soon as possible. Don't exercise for at least two days, and then start again gradually.

KNEES Most teenagers who participate in sports experience knee pain—either from overuse or from an injury.

OSGOOD-SCHLATTER DISEASE. Pain in front of the knee is common during adolescence, and generally occurs when bones are growing rapidly. If you feel a sharp pain just below the kneecap but don't remember injuring your leg, you may have Osgood-Schlatter disease, a temporary condition that usually heals by itself. Osgood-Schlatter disease is the result of small fractures of that area, where the bone grows longer during childhood and adolescence.

Your coach or trainer will probably recommend that you stay away from vigorous sports for a period of a few weeks to several months, so the area will have a chance to heal. Recurrence is rare, and you can resume your usual sports activities when the condition clears up.

SPRAINED LIGAMENT. If you suddenly twist or turn to change direction but one foot remains planted on the ground, you're likely to sprain a knee ligament. Typically, this happens in basketball, when a player pivots to avoid a defender. Most athletes who sprain knee ligaments say that the first thing they hear is a snap or a pop like a rubber band snapping at the knee joint; the bones feel as if they had suddenly separated and come back together. The knee becomes acutely painful and you can't put any weight on it. The pain subsides rather quickly, but if you try to pivot again, the knee gives out.

Anytime this happens, stop playing and apply ice to your knee immediately. Then make an appointment to see a doctor for a thorough evaluation. Many knee sprains can be treated with rest, ice, and strengthening exercises, but some may require X rays and further treatment.

CHONDROMALACIA (PATELLA-FEMORAL SYNDROME). The kneecap is a flat, triangular bone at the front of the knee that protects the joint where the thighbone meets the shinbone. Smooth cartilage that covers the back makes it easy for the kneecap to slide up and down a grooved track in the thigh bone when you bend your knee. If, for some reason, this normal, smooth tracking is disrupted, the kneecap slides in and out of the groove or rubs it, damaging the cartilage on the back of the kneecap. As a result, the cartilage becomes roughened and you feel a grinding or a sandpapery sensation when you move your knee. This condition is called chondromalacia. You're more likely to be prone to chondromalacia if you have weak quadriceps (the muscles on the front of your thighs) and tight hamstrings or if your ankles turn in when you run or walk.

Chondromalacia causes knee pain, especially when you walk. You'll also feel a grating sensation when you bend

70

your knee. To deal with the immediate pain, lie down and put a wet towel over your knee. Then put an ice pack on top of the towel and leave it there for about twenty minutes. Do this three times a day for one to three days. Check with your doctor about taking ibuprofen to control the inflammation while the injured cartilage heals. Once the pain stops, start a series of exercises to strengthen your quadriceps. Here are two:

1. Sit down on the floor, lean back on your hands, and bend the knee that isn't affected. Put a pillow under your other knee, keep that leg straight out in front of you, flex your foot so your toes point to the ceiling, and tighten your quadriceps muscles; hold for about five seconds, then relax. Start with thirty repetitions and work up to one hundred.

2. Sit in the same position but don't use a pillow. Raise your leg straight up until it's about level with the shin of your bent leg and hold it there for about five seconds. Do three sets of ten once a day.

THIGHS AND HIPS

HAMSTRING INJURIES. The hamstrings run from the buttocks down the back of the thigh. One of the most common thigh injuries that athletes experience is hamstring strain. Hamstrings are usually only three quarters as strong as quadriceps. If the quadriceps are well developed, but the hamstrings aren't, they're likely to get strained. Hamstring injuries can also result from not warming up properly, fatigue, or poor flexibility.

Hamstring strains can be mild, moderate, or severe. With a mild strain, you may not notice anything wrong until you stop playing or exercising. If the strain is moderate or severe, you'll know immediately that something is wrong; a strained hamstring feels as if you "pulled" it, or "popped" it, or "tore" it. Don't try to run through a strained hamstring. The injured muscle may bleed, causing the surrounding tissue to swell.

Treat all hamstring strains with ice and a compression wrap for the first day or two. Use an ice pack held in place with an elastic bandage for twenty minutes, three times a day. If the strain is moderate or severe, your doctor may prescribe ibuprofen or another pain reliever. Once the bleeding and swelling are under control, you can gradually begin stretching exercises.

GROIN PULL (GROIN STRAIN). If you suddenly twist or fall in such a way that you pull your inner hip muscles and feel a sudden pain in your groin, you've let yourself in for a groin strain.

Apply an ice pack as soon as possible. Your doctor may

want you to use a compression wrap for a few days. After that you'll find the strain heals faster if you do specific exercises in a hot shower or tub. Ask a coach to show you specific exercises.

CHAPTER 9

Upper-Body Injuries

You use your arms when you participate in any sport. Even runners pump their arms when they sprint or compete in a longer race. An injury to your arms or shoulders can put you on the bench for the rest of the day—or the rest of the season. And, if you participate in sports, you can injure any part of your arm from your shoulder out to the tips of your fingers.

Shoulder and Arm

You're likely to suffer a shoulder injury if you participate in any sport that involves contact with other players (football, lacrosse), that requires repeated use of a throwing or swinging motion (baseball, tennis), or if you swim.

Your shoulder is a ball-and-socket joint: The ball is the humerus, the upper end of the armbone. It sits in a socket-shaped part of your shoulder blade, the scapula,

74

which is attached to the outer end of the collarbone. A group of ligaments and muscles, called the rotator cuff, holds the humerus and scapula together. The rotator cuff lies just under the surface of the skin.

STRAINS. The most common shoulder injury is a strain, an injury to muscle fibers. Strains can be so mild that all you feel is a little soreness and tenderness that disappear within a short time. Or they can be so severe that you suffer considerable pain. If you have a mild strain, treat it with rest, ice, and compression. Start mild exercises when the pain disappears. If you have a painful strain, see a doctor.

Shoulder strains can result from one of several factors: improper technique, weak muscles, not warming up properly, or doing too much too soon, so speak to your coach or phys. ed. teacher about correcting any problems.

TENDINITIS. Tendons join the shoulder muscles to the bones. The kind of motion necessary to pitch a baseball, throw a football, or do a backstroke can inflame or tear the rotator cuff tendons, resulting in tendinitis.

Tendinitis starts out with mild pain when you move your shoulder. The pain may bother you when you start to warm up, but disappear while you're working out. Several hours after you finish working out, your shoulder becomes mildly painful again, and the pain lasts for several hours. As the tendinitis worsens, the pain no longer lets up during your workout or after you finish. Without treatment, you'll feel pain both during practice and immediately after practice. Eventually the pain becomes so bad that you can't carry books or reach for something on a high shelf.

Sometimes the tendons "impinge" upon the hard parts of the shoulder, and become irritated through being rubbed against ligaments or bone. Overuse, excessive stress, or incorrect form can all cause the type of tendinitis called impingement syndrome.

Rest, ice, and compression for three to five days eases mild tendinitis. You'll need a rehabilitation program that includes rest and exercise if the tendinitis is more severe. In a supervised exercise program, a trained professional will evaluate your athletic habits that contributed to the tendinitis, show you how to change them, and prescribe exercises to strengthen the rotator cuff so that you'll be able to avoid reinjuring yourself.

TENNIS ELBOW. Tennis elbow isn't limited to people who play tennis. If you canoe, bowl, or pitch in baseball or softball games, you're a candidate for tennis elbow— an inflammation of the tendons on the inner or outer side of the elbow. Tennis elbow results from the chronic irritation of the area near the elbow because of constant grasping and twisting motions. Overuse, poor form, or a racket strung too tightly are likely causes.

Tennis elbow begins with pain over the outer part of the elbow. If left untreated, the pain may move into the forearm. Take an anti-inflammatory painkiller such as ibuprofen and rest your arm until the pain disappears.

Ask your coach or teacher to show you the proper way

to throw, pitch, or hit to reduce the chances of a recurrence.

LITTLE LEAGUER'S ELBOW. Overuse—hours of practicing the same movements over and over—causes Little Leaguer's elbow with its symptoms of pain, tenderness, and swelling. You can best prevent it by using proper form and not overpracticing. If it does develop, don't ignore the pain or try to play through, because you risk permanent injury to your arm if you do. To minimize that risk, it's essential to rest and get professional medical advice.

Wrist and Hand

BASEBALL FINGER. If the end of your finger gets in the way of a fast-moving ball or you bang it hard against a wall or a stone, the force of the blow can separate the first joint and the tendon from the bone. If your finger hurts, you can't straighten it, and it starts to swell, you're probably suffering from baseball finger.

You may need a splint for anywhere from four to six weeks to keep your finger in place so that it heals properly. Specially designed splints permit you to continue training during that time.

DISLOCATED FINGER. A severe blow to the finger can tear the ligament, causing bones that should fit neatly alongside each other to separate. If this happens, your finger will look out of line—and will probably hurt a great deal.

If the first or second joint of the finger is dislocated,

you can try to pull it gently back into place. In any case, see a doctor. You may need an X ray to rule out a fracture.

FRACTURES OF THE HAND AND FINGERS. Athletes commonly fracture the long bones between the wrists and fingers—the metacarpals—and the finger bones— the phalanges. You'll feel pain immediately and your finger will start to swell if it is fractured.

Put an ice bag on your hand until you can get to a doctor. Generally it takes two to four weeks for a fractured finger to heal; a simple splint is usually sufficient.

NERVE COMPRESSION. Gymnasts who vault a lot or do floor exercises, and baseball catchers whose glove hand gets constantly pounded by pitches, may develop compression injuries to the nerves of the hand. The pain these injuries cause doesn't always show up in the hand itself, but may be felt as vague aches or pain on top of the wrist, weakness of the wrist, numbness, or even pain in the shoulder or neck.

Treatment begins with rest. As soon as the pain disappears, ask your coach about exercises to strengthen the wrist. If you're a gymnast, your coach will probably suggest that you tape your wrist. If you're a catcher, make sure your glove is well padded.

Breast Problems

Both boys and girls can develop breast injuries, although they more typically affect girls. Breast injuries usually aren't serious, but they can be uncomfortable.

RUNNER'S NIPPLES. Both boys and girls can develop runner's nipples, which is caused by the friction of a shirt rubbing against the nipples, usually during long-distance running. Sometimes the skin of the nipples is rubbed raw and the nipple starts bleeding. Boys often put Band-Aids over their nipples before they start running. Girls with small breasts can also use Band-Aids if bras are uncomfortable and the seams rub their nipples. Girls with larger breasts can now buy good sports bras with wide bands under the breasts and wide shoulder straps.

BREAST TRAUMA. Girls who participate in contact and racket sports risk breast injury from a blow from a ball or stick. Although these injuries may be painful, most of them aren't serious. If the breast becomes swollen and discolored, use ice and compression to minimize bleeding under the skin. If the skin is broken and the breast starts bleeding, apply direct, firm pressure to the area.

Doctors are convinced that there is no connection between a blow to the breast and the development of breast cancer, although an old wives' tale to that effect continues to be passed on from generation to generation.

Head and Face

CONCUSSION. Any violent blow to the head forces the brain to strike against the opposite side of the skull, causing a concussion—a brief malfunction and temporary swelling of the brain. Concussions are quite common, especially among participants in contact sports such as boxing, football, wrestling, and soccer.

The chief symptom of a concussion is loss of consciousness, which can last for anywhere from a few seconds to several minutes. People with concussions often complain of nausea, dizziness, headaches, tiredness, inability to concentrate, irritability, or loss of memory—symptoms that may continue for several days or weeks after the injury. Often, people with concussions can't remember what happened a few minutes before the blow. Later on, they may not be able to remember what happened a few hours after the concussion.

A mild concussion usually requires no special care, but anyone who loses consciousness following a head injury should see a doctor.

FACIAL LACERATIONS. Because the face and head are plentifully supplied with blood vessels, cuts over the eye or on the face and scalp tend to bleed a lot. This often makes these cuts appear worse than they are.

The best way to stop the bleeding is to apply pressure to the cut with a clean towel or gauze pad. You can also stop the bleeding by wrapping some ice cubes or a cupful of ice in a sterile gauze pad and holding that against the cut for a few minutes.

Until you can get to a doctor, you can tape the edges of the wound together with "butterfly" strips to help control the bleeding. A butterfly strip is a piece of tape that looks a little like a dumbbell—wide at both ends and narrow in the middle.

NOSEBLEEDS. Very few teenagers who participate in sports avoid nosebleeds, an annoying injury that's seldom serious. Noses bleed when the blood vessels in the inner lining break.

If you have a nosebleed, sit down and lean forward so the blood doesn't run back into your throat, since swallowing blood may nauseate you. If the blood flows only from one nostril, press it firmly closed with your index finger and hold it for ten minutes. If both nostrils are bleeding, breathe through your mouth while you pinch your nose closed for ten minutes with your thumb and index finger. If the nosebleed results from a direct blow to the nose, use gentle pressure. People sometimes use ice or a cold pack for a nosebleed. That may feel good, but really doesn't have much effect.

If your nose swells or changes in shape, or if the bleeding doesn't stop within twenty to thirty minutes, see a doctor.

BROKEN OR LOST TEETH. If you lose a tooth—roots and all—rinse it off, put it in a container, cover it with water, and take it to the nearest dentist. Chances are that it can be replaced in its socket and will heal in place. It's important not to let the tooth dry out. If there's no water available, put the tooth under your tongue to keep it moist.

If you chip off only part of your tooth, there's no way to reattach it. However, dentists can usually replace the missing part with a new material that fuses to the tooth.

A bloody nose or the loss of a tooth isn't all that dangerous. But some head injuries *are*—and require prompt medical attention.

FRACTURE OF THE CHEEKBONES. Because a cheekbone fracture causes little pain, it's easily overlooked. Cheekbone fractures can be dangerous, however, because the cheekbones support the eye sockets. Any damage to these bones can also damage the muscles attached to the eye. If you're hit in the face and your cheek, teeth, and upper lip become numb, you may have a fractured cheekbone. See a doctor.

FRACTURED JAW. Intense pain frequently follows a blow to the jaw, so it's difficult to tell whether or not the jaw is fractured. If you can close your upper and lower teeth together without much pain, your jaw probably isn't broken. But if your chin or lip is numb and your teeth unevenly lined up, it's more than likely that you've broken your jaw. See a doctor.

EYE INJURIES. Except for your skin, your eyes are the only organ of your body directly exposed to the world. Your eyes are therefore especially vulnerable to direct injury from balls, fingers, pucks, or sticks, as well as from dust and dirt.

A piece of grit is a tiny thing, but if it ends up in your eye, it can put you out of play in a hurry. If you get dust or dirt under your upper eyelid, gently pull your upper lid over your lower one. The tears produced by the irritation tend to make the piece of dirt stick to your lower lid, where it can be washed away. If this doesn't work, wash out your eye with sterile water. If the piece of dust or dirt is under your lower lid, use the corner edge of a sterile gauze pad to remove it.

During competition, much larger things may land in

your eye—like someone else's finger. If a fingernail scrapes the outer layer of your eyeball, it may cause what's called a corneal abrasion. It may only feel as though there's a speck of dust in your eye, but it can be serious. Any time this happens, close your eye, cover it loosely with a gauze patch, and see an eye doctor immediately.

Sometimes even larger things land in your eye—like a baseball or hockey puck. Two thirds of all eye injuries that occur to school-age youngsters are sports related, and nine out of ten of these injuries can be prevented.

Ice hockey, baseball, and racket sports such as racquetball, tennis, and badminton account for the majority of these eye injuries. And the sad truth is that most players who are injured were not wearing eye protection. The most important piece of equipment you can use to prevent eye injuries is a set of eye protectors, either masks, face guards, or safety lenses made out of polycarbonate plastic. Contact lenses, ordinary prescription eyeglasses—even those with shatterproof lenses—or lensless eye guards offer no protection.

Your coach may not insist that you wear protective gear—and a lot of other players may not wear them. But that's because a lot of other players are foolish. The loss of an eye is one of the most serious—and permanent—sports injuries you can suffer. So it pays to play it safe and protect yourself.

CHAPTER 10

Weather Extremes and Exercise

Sports injuries aren't always caused by body contact or the rigors of competition. It's all too easy to suit up with safety equipment in the locker room or buy gear to protect yourself against injury—but forget about the weather outside. Extreme weather conditions alone may cause an athlete serious trouble or injury.

Get Ready for Cold

When it's cold and windy, exercising outdoors or participating in outdoor sports can result in two potentially dangerous conditions—frostbite and hypothermia.

Nearly 65 percent of your body is made up of fluid in and around cells. In cold weather, this fluid can actually freeze, damaging, and perhaps killing, the cells themselves—a condition called FROSTBITE. Unprotected skin, such as that on fingers, toes, ears, and the exposed areas of your face, is the most likely to be frostbitten.

Frostbite is no fun—and it can cause serious damage. You've probably read about mountain climbers who lose fingers or toes as a result of frostbite. Although you probably won't risk losing a finger or toe sitting on the bench at a hockey game, you may still suffer from frostbite if you're not careful.

The warning signs of frostbite are easy to recognize. First, your skin feels extremely cold and loses its color as the blood vessels begin to close and obstruct the free flow of blood. As your body attempts to rewarm the skin, the blood vessels near the skin's surface begin to reopen in an effort to increase circulation. As this happens, your skin starts to tingle painfully or feel as if it's burning. If you don't get inside where it's warmer, the blood vessels close up again. At this point your skin feels numb and firm to the touch, and turns a peculiar yellowish-white or blue color.

Rubbing your skin when you feel chilled warms it and makes you feel better. But that doesn't work once frostbite sets in. Contrary to a popular myth, rubbing or massaging frostbitten skin with your hands or with snow only increases the risk of serious damage. Wrap the affected area with either a blanket, dry clothing, a scarf, or layers of newspaper until you can get indoors.

But even when you do get inside, it takes time for the frostbitten area to thaw. Rewarm frostbitten skin gently. Don't try to warm frostbitten skin right next to the intense heat of a fire or radiator, or in hot water—you can cause permanent damage to your skin and the area underneath. Uncover the frostbitten area and put it in water only slightly warmer than body temperature (between 100 degrees and 105 degrees Fahrenheit). It may take an hour to warm the skin, and as it warms, you'll probably see blisters start to appear. Don't break them or touch them. Cover them with a gauze bandage, if you have one, or with a clean towel or T-shirt. As soon as possible, see a doctor or go to a hospital emergency room to have the frostbitten area checked.

Overexposure to the cold can also lead to HYPOTHER-MIA—a dangerous drop in body temperature. Skiers and cyclists, in particular, risk hypothermia in cold weather—and swimmers are subject to hypothermia in any weather if they swim in cold water. As the body attempts to generate heat, the person begins to shiver uncontrolla-bly—one of the first signs of hypothermia. Confusion and slurred speech soon follow. Hypothermia is so dis-abling that even walking becomes difficult.

Because victims of hypothermia often become con-fused and disabled, teammates should be alert for these signs—and ready to help. Hypothermia is an emergency, and you must act quickly. Take your teammate to a warm shelter and remove any wet clothing. Wrap him in warm, dry blankets or clothing to gradually warm the body, and offer warm liquids to drink. As soon as possible, take him to a hospital emergency room. If he loses consciousness, go to an emergency room immediately.

It's better to prevent frostbite and hypothermia than to cope with them. One of the best ways to prevent either condition is to dress properly.

Wear several layers of loose-fitting clothing. The layers trap warm air, which helps to keep you warm. Wear clothing made of cotton or silk next to your skin; natural fibers absorb perspiration. Then add a layer of down or lightweight synthetic fabric. Top it off with a wool outer layer, since wool carries moisture away from the body. If it's windy as well as cold, add a nylon windbreaker and pants.

That takes care of your body. But surprisingly, you lose as much as half your body heat through the skin of your head. To keep warm in cold weather, you must also wear a hat—even if you have long hair. To be most effective, a hat should cover your ears as well. Because hands and feet are the first parts of the body to feel the effects of cold weather, be sure to wear long socks and mittens; mittens keep your hands warmer than gloves.

Dress warmly enough for the time you spend sitting on the bench or walking to the field. You can always shed some layers as you begin to warm up.

Hot Weather

Athletic activity combined with heat and humidity make it harder to keep cool in hot weather. Athletes can develop heat cramps, heat exhaustion, or heat stroke from working out in hot weather. In hot weather, the body cools itself through sweat evaporation. But as the humidity climbs and the outside temperature rises above your normal body temperature (98.6 degrees), the sweat stops evaporating and the outside heat begins to raise your body temperature.

Exercising in hot, humid weather can cause HEAT CRAMPS—sudden sharp cramps in your arms, legs, or abdomen. The severe cramping makes the muscles feel like hard knots. Heat cramps may come on during a workout, or they may develop several hours afterward. No one is quite sure what brings them on, although scientists generally believe that heat cramps probably result from the loss of body salt through excessive sweating. In most cases, you can relieve heat cramps quickly by taking a drink of water and eating a few salted potato chips. Stretch out the cramped muscle, but don't knead it or massage it. Massage usually makes it worse. If you're prone to heat cramps, make sure you drink enough water during warm weather and try eating more potassium-rich food (such as bananas, oranges, and peanut butter) and more salty food—but don't take salt tablets unless your doctor recommends them.

HEAT EXHAUSTION, an excessive loss of body salt and fluid, usually occurs during exercise in very hot, humid weather. Symptoms are profuse sweating, nausea, dizziness, faintness, moist and clammy skin, and light-headedness. The best treatment for heat exhaustion is to rest in a cool place and drink cold water. Take it easy for the rest of the day and stay out of the heat.

HEAT STROKE generally occurs during prolonged exertion in hot, humid weather when the body's internal cooling mechanism breaks down. People used to distinguish between heat stroke and heat exhaustion by whether the victim was perspiring, because victims of heat stroke usually don't sweat. But that's not a valid distinction, because some victims of heat stroke do sweat. In either case, their skin feels hot to the touch, they feel feverish, and their body temperature soars. Victims of heat stroke also act oddly; they may hallucinate or seem confused. Heat stroke is a life-threatening condition and a medical emergency. Call for medical help at once. While waiting for an ambulance, take off all the athlete's clothing and cool the body as quickly as possible by sponging with cold water or ice cubes.

SUNBURN. If you exercise or play outdoors, you risk getting sunburned—a skin burn caused by overexposure to ultraviolet radiation from the sun. You can get sunburned in winter as well as summer—as you well know if you ski or climb mountains. Sunburn causes inflammation, swelling, pain, and redness of the skin, usually about four to six hours after exposure to sunlight. We know that radiation from sunlight permanently damages the skin. The damage can include leathery, wrinkled skin and an increased chance of skin cancer. Suntans damage the skin less severely—but some damage does occur.

The best thing you can do to protect your skin is to use a sunscreen. Sunscreens chemically absorb the damaging part of the sun's ultraviolet radiation. Sunscreens have a sun-protection factor (SPF) of anywhere from 2 to 30; the higher the number, the greater the protection. The SPF tells you how much longer you can stay in the sun without getting burned if you use the sunscreen than if you don't. For instance, if you can usually stay in the sun without any protection for half an hour before you start to turn pink, a sunscreen with an SPF of 8 will protect you for four hours, a sunscreen with an SPF of 4 will protect you for two hours. Obviously, you have to know something about your own skin to use a sunscreen intelligently. Doctors now recommend sunscreens with an SPF of 15 or above. Anything less won't give needed protection.

Use a sunscreen whether you're fair or dark. The most effective sunscreens are those that contain PABA (para-aminobenzoic acid) and benzophenones. PABA absorbs ultraviolet B rays, the rays responsible for many of the changes that result in burning and increased risk of skin cancer. Benzophenones absorb ultraviolet A rays, which, to a lesser extent, produce burning and skin cancer. Put on sunscreen about thirty to forty-five minutes before you go into the sun, and check the label to see how often you have to reapply it.

What if you do get a sunburn? The best way to relieve the pain is to soak in a tub of cool water. If only your face is burned, use a washcloth wrung out in plain, cool water. Calamine lotion will help to soothe and cool your skin, but don't use any other preparations sold to relieve sunburn, because they often cause allergic skin reactions that make you feel even worse.

When the burn is at its worst, take ibuprofen (such as Advil or Medipren)—but don't exceed the recommended dose.

After a severe sunburn your skin will peel—and there's nothing to prevent that from happening. Baby oil or moisturizer will make your skin feel less rough, but won't stop the peeling.

Prevention

You can prevent all these hot-weather problems with some common-sense precautions:

In extreme hot weather, work out or practice during the cooler hours of the day—early morning and late afternoon if possible.

Leave yourself time to adapt to exercising in hot weather. The process of adapting is called acclimatization, which takes a week or two. Start out with light, short sessions with plenty of rest between them. Gradually work up to longer, more strenuous ones.

Wear white or light-colored clothing made of lightweight fabrics that fit loosely at the neck, waist, and sleeves. Mesh shirts are particularly good.

Include fruits and green salads in your diet to help replace the body salts you lose through sweating.

Always use a sunscreen with a high SPF, whether it's sunny or not. You can get sunburned on cloudy, hazy days because ultraviolet rays can still come through.

It may be fun to run through a sprinkler to cool off on a hot day, but water on your skin won't prevent heat stress. It's more important to *drink* enough water.

Water

Water carries nutrients to cells, and carries away waste products from cells. Water also absorbs internal body heat from muscles and transports it to the skin, cooling the body through the formation and secretion of sweat—

particularly important for athletes.

Dehydration (the loss of body water) is the main problem associated with exercising in hot weather. Probably the most important—and most overlooked—factor in any exercise program is water. Other animals instinctively drink enough water to replace what they lose—but human beings don't. Humans often drink only enough to take the edge off thirst, not enough to replace all lost fluids.

At the very least, drink two glasses of plain water before you start to exercise, and one glass every fifteen minutes during hot-weather exercise or training sessions.

Don't forget about drinking water during winter workouts as well. You're just as likely to become dehydrated during the winter on a basketball court or indoor track as you are in the summer when you're on the playing field.

You may not sweat as much indoors in winter, but in cold weather you lose water through your lungs. The air outside and in heated buildings is almost always drier in winter than in summer. Before your lungs can absorb air, your body must heat and moisturize it. That uses up a lot of body fluid. If you lose as little as 2 percent of your body weight through dehydration, your performance will suffer. If you lose any more than that, your strength and aerobic capacity will be reduced.

CHAPTER 11

Drugs

It's nice to think that you can gain an athletic edge just by swallowing something, taking an injection, or inhaling a "magic" substance. And, in fact, many athletes try to do just that. They put their faith in ergogenic aids, substances supposed to help them generate greater force or endurance, and increase their ability to exercise harder. Some ergogenic aids, such as bee pollen, brewer's yeast, or wheat germ oil, are harmless—but they're also worthless. Others, the ones we refer to as drugs, are sometimes effective, frequently illegal, and often dangerous.

The use of drugs may increase muscle strength, delay fatigue, and stimulate the nervous system. And some— such as caffeine—are relatively risk free. But you may risk much more by using others—such as steroids. The old adage that you can't get something for nothing holds as true for drugs as for anything else. Any drug that improves athletic performance also carries with it some cost.

Drugs that promise easy, short-term gains won't lead to a long-term payoff. Maintaining a drug habit can be a distraction from concentrating on your sport, and eats up a lot of money and time that could better be spent in training. In the end, there's no substitute for practice, good technique, good coaching, and hard work.

The use of drugs may be illegal and often raises serious questions about morality and fair play, but those issues lie outside the scope of this book. This chapter deals only with the impact of some drugs on athletic performance and health.

Caffeine

Caffeine is one of the least dangerous and most widely used of a group of drugs called psychomotor stimulants, which delay fatigue and speed reaction time—obviously both advantages in athletic performance.

Caffeine is so readily and legally available that most people never think of it as a drug. It occurs naturally in coffee, tea, colas, chocolate, and cocoa, and is often added to over-the-counter medications to prevent drowsiness.

Individual sensitivity to caffeine varies greatly. Some people are so sensitive to its effects that they react to just one cup of coffee with rapid heartbeat, jitters, stomach cramps, and insomnia. Others drink two or three cups of coffee before bed and still sleep soundly through the night.

Everyone knows that caffeine can help to keep you wide awake and alert. The fact that caffeine can improve performance during endurance events such as marathons is less familiar. During these events, the body first burns free fatty acids for energy and then draws on muscle glycogen stores. The glycogen provides the backup reserves of energy, and the longer those reserves remain unused, the longer you can hold out before you begin to feel exhausted. Caffeine raises the level of free fatty acids in the blood, so the body can burn them and spare the glycogen reserves. This glycogen-sparing effect helps only in endurance events; caffeine does not improve performance for shorter events.

Studies of both athletes and nonathletes have shown that the amount of caffeine in two and a half cups of coffee increased their endurance and maximal oxygen consumption. Small doses of caffeine also significantly increased the power of leg muscle contractions.

Does this mean you should drink as much coffee as possible before a marathon? No. Too much coffee can make you so jittery you lose concentration, and too much coffee also means more pit stops. Although moderate amounts of caffeine are safe, coffee, tea, and cola stimulate the flow of urine and the urge to urinate—which can be uncomfortable and distracting during competition.

A cup of brewed coffee contains between 100 and 150 milligrams (mg.) of caffeine, a cup of tea contains approximately 20 to 50 mg. of caffeine, most cola drinks contain between 35 and 75 mg. of caffeine in each 12-ounce serving, and a cup of cocoa contains 50 mg. of caffeine.

The International Olympics Committee classifies caffeine as a drug and has limited the amount permissible in urine to 12 micrograms of caffeine per milliliter of urine. Two cups of brewed coffee produce urine levels of 6 micrograms per milliliter.

Tobacco

Some athletes smoke a cigarette to calm their nerves before an event. Others smoke for just the opposite reason—as a stimulant to focus attention. The trouble is that smokers get drawn into a vicious cycle and need another cigarette to stay either calm or alert—and that can interfere with concentration during the game.

Tobacco is as readily and legally available as coffee. By now, however, everyone knows about the serious long-term consequences of cigarette smoking. Smoking tobacco causes lung and other cancers, emphysema, and heart disease in the long run. But even in the short run, cigarette smoking impairs athletic performance.

Most people are aware that smokers become winded sooner than nonsmokers, but without knowing why.

Nicotine, the active ingredient in tobacco, is a stimulant. Nicotine acts on specific nerves in the body, stimulating them to release chemicals that narrow blood vessels, increase heart rate, and raise blood pressure.

Cigarette smoke also contains carbon monoxide, which interferes with the ability of red blood cells to carry oxygen. Together, nicotine and carbon monoxide deliver a double whammy to the oxygen supply that guarantees that a smoker will not be able to perform as well in athletic competition as a nonsmoker.

So it isn't surprising that study after study shows that smoking impairs physical performance. Smokers use more energy simply to breathe, their resting heart rate is higher, and their oxygen uptake decreases during exercise testing. Smokers also have more minor health problems. And they don't sleep as well or as long as nonsmokers. Obviously, this can hamper athletic performance since fatigue is one of the worst enemies of any athlete, and it's difficult to avoid fatigue without enough sleep.

Some people try to avoid the dangers of smoking by using "smokeless tobacco," which is another name for chewing tobacco. But chewing tobacco is just as addictive as cigarettes and delivers high levels of nicotine to the body, absorbed through the mucous lining of the mouth.

Contrary to its image as safe for athletes, smokeless tobacco slows reaction time and raises blood pressure. During exercise, it decreases the amount of blood the heart can pump, reducing the flow of oxygen to muscles that need it.

Cocaine

Cocaine, an old drug that's found new popularity, can be extracted from the coca plant. Some South American Indians chew the leaves to release the cocaine, which acts as a stimulant. At one time, only the Inca aristocracy was permitted to chew the coca leaves, but after the Spanish conquest, the Spaniards encouraged the enslaved Indians to use it so they could endure long periods of heavy labor and physical hardship.

Athletes are likely to be attracted to cocaine because it produces a "high" that promotes a feeling of alertness and well-being.

Researchers haven't studied the effects of cocaine on athletic performance in particular. But cocaine does throw off judgment and may even cause the user to believe that everyone's out to get her. Besides, cocaine acts as an anesthetic as well as a stimulant. Moderate doses increase the heart rate and affect the central nervous system. Large doses may even result in coma, convulsions, or death.

People who use cocaine generally "snort" it—inhale it through the nose in the form of a powder. Cocaine can also be converted to "free-base" so it can be inhaled like cigarette smoke. In free-base smoking, a cocaine extract is prepared with the use of a solvent, such as ether. Crack, a recently developed, almost pure form of cocaine, can be smoked either in a pipe or mixed with tobacco in a cigarette.

Cocaine can mask a sense of fatigue, leaving you open

to injury. Cocaine also leaves you irritable, agitated, restless, and depressed when its effects wear off. Cocaine can also change your behavior in strange ways, so that work habits and relationships suffer.

Marijuana

Athletes always want to be "up" for a game, and sometimes think they'll play better on a marijuana high. Marijuana is a hallucinogen, a drug that alters the way you perceive reality by interfering with the way your brain works. Marijuana usually produces feelings of relaxation and euphoria. But while that effect might set you up psychologically for competition, for most users it also distorts perceptions of distance and time, which is not at all what you need for top performance in any sport.

The effects of one joint can last for two or three hours. Not only that, but it tends to linger in your system for a long time. The active ingredient in marijuana is delta-9 tetrahydrocannabinol (THC), which is fat soluble. That is, fat cells and organs soak it up after it enters the bloodstream, and it accumulates in body fat. Because THC remains in the body for up to thirty days, even if you smoke only one joint a week, you have a constant, active level of THC in your body.

Daily use of marijuana leads to lung damage. Smoking less than one joint a day affects vital capacity (the amount of air you can exhale from your lungs after a deep breath) as much as smoking sixteen cigarettes a day.

To study the effects of marijuana smoking on exercise,

99

researchers had young men and women perform progressive exercise tests on a cycle ergometer twenty minutes after smoking a marijuana cigarette. They also performed the test without smoking marijuana. Smoking marijuana significantly decreased their work capacity as well as increased their preexercise heart rate.

Marijuana also adversely affects coordination, muscle strength, reaction time, judgment, short-term memory, and concentration—all of which impair athletic performance.

There can also be some unwanted secondary effects. Men who use marijuana heavily have lower levels of testosterone, a male sex hormone, than average. At these lower levels, female sex characteristics, such as enlarged breasts, may develop.

Alcohol

If your stomach is tied in knots before a game, it's tempting to take a beer or two to relax. But although it's tempting, it's not wise. A beer or two before a game will hurt your performance rather than help it.

Alcohol is a central-nervous-system depressant, and that means that it reduces alertness, impairs motor coordination, and slows reaction time. Alcohol also impairs judgment and affects perception, so that you think your senses are sharp when in fact they're faulty. In the same way that coffee does, alcohol stimulates the urge to urinate and the flow of urine. These are all good reasons not to have that beer to relax before the game.

If you do drink too much, neither cold showers nor coffee will sober you up. Alcohol is eliminated from the bloodstream by the liver, and it takes about an hour for the body to get rid of an ounce of hard liquor. That's the equivalent of a jigger of whiskey, or eight to twelve ounces of beer, or four ounces of wine.

Steroids

Athletes use steroids to become stronger and build bigger muscles. Some athletes also believe that steroids enable them to train harder and recuperate more quickly. Steroid use is most often associated with football players, track athletes, weightlifters and bodybuilders—but some teenagers are taking them "just to look better." Sounds like magic—but what are they?

Steroid is the chemical name for a group of compounds that is widely distributed in nature and that includes many hormones and certain natural drugs. Humans produce two main types of steroids—cortical and anabolic. Cortical steroids are formed in the cortex (the outside) of the two adrenal glands, one located on top of each kidney. Doctors use cortical steroids to treat a wide variety of allergic conditions, control inflammation, counter serious attacks of asthma, and manage some serious skin disorders. Anabolic steroids promote tissue growth. They are used to treat certain rare types of anemia, some skin disorders, severe burns, and delayed sexual development.

When athletes talk about "using steroids," they're re-

101

ferring to a synthetic form of one of the anabolic steroids: the male hormone testosterone. Testosterone triggers the masculine changes that occur during puberty, among them lower voice, growth of body and facial hair, and maturation of the penis and testes.

Do steroids work? In fact, they do—to some degree. The debate centers around the long-term effect of steroid use—especially when taken in large doses. Researchers agree that when normal, healthy adult men take steroids without training, they have no effect on muscle strength or size. But steroids can build bigger and stronger muscles when taken in low doses and supplemented with a well-balanced diet and an established weight-training program. So what's the problem?

First of all, steroids don't work the same way for everyone. One weightlifter may bulk up on the same dose of the same drug that doesn't do a thing for his friend. Second, most athletes on steroids take four to eight times the recommended medical dose and "stack" them, taking two or three different drugs simultaneously in cycles that last anywhere from one week to thirteen weeks or more.

Some doctors contend that current studies on the consequences of steroid use don't prove anything about their effect on athletes because the research doesn't reflect the large doses that are common in illegal use—and researchers are not permitted to give their test subjects such large doses. In addition, because the drugs haven't been studied long enough, there is no conclusive scientific evidence regarding long-term health effects.

But although we won't have conclusive results for many years, researchers do link steroid use to several long-term side effects. Steroids damage the kidneys and cause liver disorders. Steroid use may also contribute to eventual heart disease, stemming from a combination of high blood pressure and an increased level of fats in the blood.

Most of the studies on the health risks of steroids have dealt with adults. Some of the changes steroids bring about may be reversible or may not matter to an adult, but the consequences for teenagers can be permanent and could matter a great deal.

Most troublesome for teenagers are side effects that affect growth and sexual functioning. Steroids cause the growing tips of the long bones to close prematurely, stunting the growth of teenagers who take the drugs before they reach their full height. Less permanent, but still worrisome, steroids often cause acne.

Steroids also cause changes in both the male and female reproductive systems. While taking synthetic steroids may increase muscle size, it suppresses the body's own production of sex hormones. As a result, sperm production decreases in boys, the testes shrink and breasts grow, and achieving and maintaining an erection is more difficult. In girls, the addition of male hormones causes menstrual periods to stop, the clitoris to enlarge, and breasts to shrink. Other distressing masculinizing effects include the growth of facial and chest hair and a deepened voice.

Not all the effects of steroids are physical. "Roid

rage"—violent mood swings, irritability, and uncontrollable aggressive behavior—frequently accompanies steroid use.

Human Growth Hormone

Human growth hormone (hGH), secreted by the pituitary gland, is essential for normal growth. Doctors use growth hormone to treat very short children, enabling them to achieve normal height.

Several years ago, distribution of naturally occurring growth hormone was halted voluntarily because the drug was thought to be contaminated with a virus that causes an inevitably fatal disease with symptoms that include irreversible mental deterioration. More recently, a synthetic growth hormone has been developed that does not have this side effect.

The illicit use of hGH is too new to document any side effects, but don't even think of taking it unless your doctor prescribes it for a legitimate, medically approved reason.

Special Terms

aerobic capacity—the maximum rate at which the body uses oxygen.

aerobic exercise—conditioning that improves circulation by expanding blood vessels and increasing oxygen consumption.

aerobic system—the parts of the body that collectively use oxygen to provide energy for prolonged activity.

alcohol—a central-nervous-system depressant.

anaerobic system—the parts of the body that collectively provide immediate energy for sudden, intense activity without using oxygen.

athlete's foot—a fungal infection of the foot that causes redness as well as cracking and peeling skin between the toes.

blister—an accumulation of fluid between skin layers that develops when skin is rubbed repeatedly.

burnout—loss of energy and enthusiasm for a sport.

caffeine —a psychomotor stimulant that delays fatigue and speeds reaction time.

calorie —a measure of the amount of energy (in the form of heat) that the body can produce from a food substance.

carbohydrate loading —packing muscles with glycogen stores before an endurance event to increase endurance.

carbohydrates —compounds that contain carbon, oxygen, and hydrogen, including starches and sugars.

cardiovascular endurance —the ability of the heart, lungs, and circulatory system to work together to deliver oxygen to the body's cells and to take away waste products.

charley horse —a painful muscle spasm of the thigh caused by a kick, fall, or sharp blow.

chondromalacia —damaged cartilage on the back of the kneecap that causes a grinding or sandpapery sensation when the knee is moved.

cocaine —a drug extracted from the coca plant that acts as a stimulant.

concussion —an injury to the brain resulting from a severe blow to the head.

cool-down —a tapering off of activities to enable the body to return to its resting state gradually.

cramp —a local muscle spasm.

fast-twitch muscle fibers —muscle fibers that provide rapid movement for short periods. Fast-twitch fibers generate powerful contractions needed for pitching, throwing, and jumping.

106

fat —a substance that provides energy and helps with absorption of fat-soluble vitamins.

flexibility —the range of movement of muscles and joints.

fracture —a break in a bone.

frostbite —tissue damage that results from freezing due to lack of blood circulation; usually affects fingers, toes, and ears.

glucose —the main source of energy in humans; stored in the form of glycogen in the liver and in muscle tissue, and converted back into glucose when needed.

glycogen —the form in which the body stores reserve energy.

hamstring —muscle that runs from the buttocks down the back of the thigh.

heat cramps —sudden, sharp pains in arms, legs, or abdomen that develop during hot-weather exercise.

heat stroke —a potentially life-threatening breakdown of the body's internal cooling mechanism characterized by extremely high body temperature and confusion.

heel spur —a small, bumpy outgrowth of bone under the heel.

human growth hormone (hGH) —a hormone essential for normal growth, secreted by the pituitary gland.

hypertrophy —increase in muscle size resulting from increased activity.

hypothermia —a dangerous drop in body temperature.

isokinetic exercise —a specialized type of isotonic exercise that involves work against resistance provided by a machine.

isometric exercise —a type of exercise that causes muscle tension with no body movement. Pushing against a wall is an isometric exercise.

isotonic exercise —a type of exercise that causes muscle contraction through movement. Lifting free weights is an isotonic exercise.

jock itch —an infection that causes a burning, painful, itchy rash affecting the groin.

lactic acid —a chemical waste that causes fatigue and interferes with efficient muscle function.

marijuana —a hallucinogen, a drug that alters the way you perceive reality by interfering with the way the brain works.

minerals —inorganic compounds that contribute to energy production and body maintenance.

muscle —a specialized tissue that has the ability to produce force or movement.

muscle endurance —a muscle's ability to repeat the same movement.

muscle strength —the greatest force a muscle can produce—once.

Osgood-Schlatter disease —a temporary condition that causes sharp pain just below the kneecap.

plantar fasciitis —inflammation of the band of tissue that runs along the bottom of the foot.

progressive resistance training (also called strength training) —a program of exercise that develops strong, more efficient muscles through exercises that slowly increase the amount of resistance you work against.

proteins —complex compounds made up of amino

acids; most of the body's tissues, especially muscles, are composed of protein.

RICE—an acronym for *r*est, *i*ce, *c*ompression, and *e*levation, used to treat minor injuries and limit swelling.

shin splint—a throbbing pain along the lower leg, especially along the shin.

slow-twitch muscle fibers—muscle fibers that contract slowly and provide energy for prolonged periods. Slow-twitch fibers help maintain posture and are important for endurance sports such as long-distance running and cross-country skiing.

spasm—a prolonged, painful muscle contraction.

sprain—an injury to a ligament, the connection between two bones.

steroids—the chemical name for a group of compounds that includes many hormones and certain natural drugs. Cortical steroids, formed in the cortex of the adrenal glands, are used to treat allergic conditions, control inflammation, and manage some serious skin disorders. Anabolic steroids promote tissue growth and are used to treat certain types of anemia, severe burns, and delayed sexual development.

stitch—a sharp, sudden pain in the abdomen near the lower rib cage.

strain—an injury to muscle fibers.

stress fracture—a hairline crack in a bone; it usually occurs in the feet or legs.

stretching—slowly pulling muscles to full extension to increase flexibility and suppleness.

sunburn—a skin burn caused by overexposure to ultraviolet radiation from the sun.

tendinitis—painful inflammation of a tendon, usually resulting from overuse or pressure.

tennis elbow—a painful inflammation of the tendons on the inner or outer side of the elbow.

turf toe—an injury caused by suddenly jamming the big toe forward.

vitamins—a group of required organic substances not manufactured by the body; help to convert food to living tissue.

warm-up—a technique that prepares the body for exercise by warming muscles and tendons, increasing blood flow to muscles, increasing heart and pulse rates, and raising internal temperature to ideal level for peak performance.

Index

abdomen, 5, 56–57
acclimatization, 91
Achilles tendon, 68
adrenal glands, 101
aerobic system
    capacity, 9, 92
    conditioning, 9–10
    definition of, 3, 8
    exercise, 3, 8–10, 16
    slow-twitch muscle fibers, 13
agonist muscles, 12
alcohol, 100–1
amino acids, 20
anabolic steroids, 101
anaerobic system
    definition of, 8
    exercise, 8–10
    fast-twitch muscle fibers, 13
    threshold, 9
anemia, 28, 48, 101
ankles
    exercise, 31, 70
    injury to, 61, 65–66

antagonist muscles, 12
arms
    exercise, 16, 33, 36–40, 43, 74
    injury to, 74–77
aspirin, 64
athletes, professional
    "burn" and, 6–7
    carbohydrate loading and, 22
athlete's foot (tinea pedis), 53–54

back, exercise, 31, 37, 39–40
bacteria, 54–55
badminton, 83
baseball, 1, 2, 9, 32, 62, 74–76, 78, 83
baseball finger, 77
basketball, 16, 32, 62, 69, 72
bench press, 16
benzophenones, 90
biceps, 12, 13
bicycling. See cycling
blisters, 55–56
blood. See circulatory system

bones
  collarbone, 75
  humerus, 74
  injury to, 62, 64, 66–68
  metacarpal, 78
  pelvic, 41
  phalanges, 78
  scapula, 74–75
  tibia, 66
bouncing, 32, 35
bowling, 76
boxing, vii, 79
brain, 11, 64, 79
breasts, injury to, 78–79
breathing, 34–35, 40, 57
"burn," 6–7
burnout, 44–49
butterfly strip, 80
buttocks, 15
  See also hamstrings

caffeine, 93–96, 100–101
calamine lotion, 90
calcium, 19, 28
calf muscles, 13, 43, 57, 66
calisthenics, 31, 35
calories, 19–20
  definition of, 19
  empty, 20, 24–25
canoeing, 76
carbohydrates, 17–25, 27
  complex, 21, 27
  definition of, 18
  diet, 18–21
  loading, 22–25
  measurement of, 21
  muscles and, 18, 21
  refined and unrefined, 19–20
carbon monoxide, 97

cardiovascular endurance
  definition of, 2–3
  fitness and, 2
  performance and, 3, 9
cartilage, 70
charley horse, 57–58
cheekbones, fracture of, 82
chin-ups, 4, 16
chondromalacia (patella-femoral
  syndrome), 70–71
circulatory system, 2–3, 7–13, 18,
  25–27, 30, 33, 58, 61, 72, 80,
  85, 97–98, 103
clothing
  cold weather and, 86–87
  hot weather and, 91
coaches, vii, ix, 4, 6, 10, 15, 46, 47,
  49, 69, 73, 75, 78, 83, 94
cocaine, 98–99
commitment, 44–46
competition, 47–50
compression, for minor injury, 59,
  62, 65, 72–73, 75–76, 79
concentration, 44–45, 100
concussion, 79–80
conditioning, 4, 8
  aerobic, 8
  strength training program, 4
cool-down, 33–34, 57
core exercises
  bench press, 16
  lower body, 16
  power clean, 16
  squat, 15–16
corneal abrasion, 83
cortical steroids, 101
crack, 98
cramps
  heat, 88

muscle spasm, 57–58
stomach, 25–27, 94
cycling, 3–5, 10, 16, 34, 86

dehydration, 25, 92
developmental stretch, 31
diet, vii, 17–28, 56, 91
digestion, 11, 18–20, 26–27
discus, vii
doctors, ix, 48, 61–62, 64–65, 70,
   72, 75, 78, 80–83, 86, 88–89
drugs, 93–104
   alcohol, 100–101
   caffeine, 94–96
   cocaine, 98–99
   crack, 98
   human growth hormone (hGH),
      104
   marijuana, 99–100
   steroids, 101–4
   tobacco, 96–97
dumbbells, 16

ears, injury to, 84–86
elbows, injury to, 76–77
electrolytes, 26
elevation, for minor injury, 58–59,
   62, 65
emotions, effect on performance,
   44–52
endurance, 13–14
   carbohydrate loading and, 22
   cardiovascular, 2–5
   conditioning and, 4
   definition of, 3
   development of, 16
   event, preparation for, 22–25, 95
   long- and short-term, 4
   muscle, 2–5, 13, 16

short-term, 4
   training, 4, 14
energy
   calories, as measurement of, 19
   diet and, 18–19
   exercise and, 8–9
exercise, 3–5, 12–16, 23
   aerobic, 3
   anaerobic, 8–10
   ballistic stretching, 32
   core, 15–16
   endurance training, 4, 14, 23
   isokinetic, 12
   isometric, 12
   isotonic, 12–13
   lower-body, 16
   machines, 13, 15
   repetition, 4, 15
   strength training (progressive
      resistance training), 4, 14–16
   stretching, 5, 31–32, 68
   upper-body, 16, 38–40
   See also ankles; arms; back;
      hamstrings; knees; legs
eyes, injury to, 82–83

fat, 5–6
   in diet, 17–21
   measurement of, 6
   need for, 5, 18–19
   percentage of body weight, 5
   steroids and, 103
   stomach cramps and, 27
fatigue, 7, 9–10, 22, 27, 33, 46, 72,
   80, 98–99
feet, injury to, 53–54, 60–65
fibers, muscle, 11, 13
fingers, injury to, 77–78
fitness, 1–7

113

flexibility
  definition of, 5
  development of, 5
  fitness and, 2
  warm-up and, 30–32
food. *See* diet
food groups, 23
football, 3, 5, 9, 13, 32, 62, 74–75, 79
fracture, 66–69
  ankle, 66
  cheekbone, 82
  hand and finger, 78
  knee, 69
  jaw, 82
  shin splint, 66
  stress, 67–68
frostbite, 84–86
fungus, 53–55

glucose (blood sugar), 18, 21
glycogen, 18, 21, 25, 27, 95
groin pull (groin strain), 72–73
gymnastics, 5, 60, 78

hamstrings
  exercise, 40–42, 70
  injury to, 72
hands, injury to, 77–78
head, exercise, 36
head and face, injury to, 79–83
  cheekbone fracture, 82
  concussion, 79–80
  lacerations, 80
  nosebleed, 80–81
  tooth injury, 81
heart. *See* circulatory system
heat cramps, 87–88
heat exhaustion, 25, 88
heat stroke, 88–89

heel spur syndrome (plantar
  fasciitis), 63–65
heels, injury to, 62–65
heredity, muscle fiber and, 14
hips
  exercise, 15–16, 31, 37, 40–42
  injury to, 72–73
human growth hormone (hGH),
  104
humerus, 74–75
hurdling, 62
hypertrophy. *See* overload
hypothermia, 86–87

ibuprofen, 64, 68, 71–72, 76, 90
ice, 58–59, 62, 64–65, 67–68,
  70–72, 75–76, 78–80, 89
ice hockey, 83
imagery, mental, 51–52
impingement syndrome, 76
injury, 56–86, 90
  ankle, 61, 65–66
  arm, 74–77
  bone, 62, 64, 66–68
  breast, 78–79
  "burn" and, 7
  burnout and, 47
  feet, 61–65, 84–86
  hand, 77–78
  head and face, 79–83
  hip, 72–73
  jaw, 82
  joint, 5
  leg, 66–73
  ligament, 69–70, 75, 77
  lower body, 60–73
  muscle, 5, 14–15, 57–58, 69
  prevention of, 4–5, 14–15, 30, 35,
    62–63, 90

114

shoulder, 74–75
skin, 53, 56–59, 84–86
stretching and, 32
teeth, 81
upper body, 74–83
wrist, 77–78

jaw, fracture of, 82
jogging, 31, 34–35, 67
joints, 5, 30–31, 74
jumping, 13, 16, 22

kidneys, 20, 102, 103
knees
exercise, 31, 37–38, 40–43
injury to, 69–71

lacerations, facial, 80
lacrosse, 74
lactic acid, 9, 33
legs
exercise, 16, 31, 33, 38, 40–43,
60, 71
injury to, 66–73
ligaments
definition of, 65
healthy, 2, 14
injury to, 69–70, 75, 77
Little Leaguer's elbow, 77
liver, 20, 103
loading. See carbohydrates
lower body
exercise, 16, 40–43
injury to, 60–73
lungs, 2–3, 9, 12–13, 92

machines, exercise, 13, 15
marathon, 8, 95
marijuana, 99–100

massage, 85, 88
minerals, 17–18, 24, 27–28
motivation, 46–49
mountain climbing, 89
muscle, 11–16, 29–35, 40–43,
69–70, 100, 104
agonist, 12
anaerobic, 9
antagonist, 12
biceps, 12, 13
calf, 13, 43, 57
cold, 5, 32, 35
cool-down, 33–34
diet and, 18, 26
endurance, 2–5, 13, 16
fiber, 11, 13, 15
function, 11–12
groups, 15
hamstring, 40–42, 70, 72
injury to, 5, 32, 57–58
involuntary, 11
overload, 14–15
paired, 11–12
power, 14, 16, 30, 104
protein and, 15, 20
pulls, 69
quadriceps, 41, 70, 72
size, 14–15, 20
skeletal, 11
spasm, 57–58
speed of movement, 13–14, 30
strength, 2–4, 13–14, 16, 20, 100
striated, 11
triceps, 12, 13
voluntary, 11
warm, 5, 32
warm-up and, 29–32, 35

nausea, 22, 24, 80–81, 88

neck, 31, 80
nerves, 11, 30, 78, 96–97
nicotine, 96–97
"No pain, no gain," 6, 31–32
nosebleeds, 80–81
nutrition. *See* diet

orthotics (contoured foot supports),
   67
Osgood-Schlatter, disease, 69
overload of muscles, 7, 14–15
oxygen, 3, 7–9, 13–14, 33, 95, 97

PABA (paraaminobenzoic acid), 90
pain, 6–7, 31–33, 53–59, 61–72,
   75–82
pancreas, 25
pelvic bone, 41
performance, 25–27
   cardiovascular endurance, 3
   diet, 17–18, 20, 26–27, 94–100
   emotions, 44–46, 49–51
   energy, 8
   sweating, 25, 92
   warm-up, 29
posture, 13
potassium, 26, 88
power clean, 16
preparation, mental, 50–51
pressure, psychological, 47–48
progressive overload. *See* overload
progressive resistance training. *See*
   strength training
protective gear, 83
protein
   diet, 17–21, 23–24
   measurement of, 21
   muscles and, 15, 20
   need for, 17

stomach cramps and, 27
psychology of sports, 44–52
psychomotor stimulants, 94
push-aways, 68
push-ups, 4, 12, 16

quadriceps, 41, 70–72

race walking, 10
racquetball, 83
rehabilitation, 65, 76
repetition, 4, 15–16
resistance, 14–16
rest, 15, 32, 58, 62, 67, 69–70,
   75–78, 88
Reye's syndrome, 64
RICE (rest, ice, compression, and
   elevation), 58–59, 62
"Roid rage," 103–4
rope jumping and skipping, 2, 10,
   31, 35
rotator cuff, 75
runner's nipples, 79
running, vii, 2–5, 8, 11, 13, 34, 64,
   66–68, 70, 92

salt, 26, 88
scapula, 74–75
second pull stretch, 31
self-image, 50–51
shin splints (medial tribial
   syndrome), 66–67
shoes, 54, 56, 62–68
shoulders
   exercises, 15–16, 36, 38–39
   injury to, 74–76, 78
sit-ups, 4, 16
skating, 3
skeletal muscles, 11

skiing, 10, 13, 86, 89

skin, 53–56, 59, 84–86, 103

small intestine, 25–26

soccer, 1, 32, 62, 79

socks, 54, 56

sodium. *See* salt

softball, 76

spasm (of muscle), 57–58

SPF (sun-protection factor), 89–91

spirit, 44, 46–49

sprain, 65

sprinting, 8–10, 13, 50

spurs. *See* heel spur syndrome

squat, 15–16

stamina. *See* endurance, muscle

steroids, 93, 101–4

stitch

    abdomen, 56–57

    hamstrings, 72

    stomach, 11, 25–26, 94

strain, 75

strength, 2–3, 13–16

    definition of, 3

    dehydration and, 92

    muscle, 13–14, 16, 100

    upper body, 16

strength training (progressive

    resistance training), 4, 14–16

stress, 30, 47–48

stress fracture, 67

stretching

    back, 39–40

    calves, 43

    cool-down, 33–34

    cramped muscles, 57

    duration, 35

    exercises, 5, 23, 31, 36–43, 65,

      68, 72

    first pull, 31

    function of, 35

    general, 36–38

    hamstrings, 34, 41–42

    hips, 40–41

    lower-body, 40

    quadriceps, 41–42

    thighs, 34

    upper-body, 38–39

    warm-up, 31–32, 35

sunburn, 89–91

sweating, 25, 31, 87–89, 91–92

swimming, 2–3, 5, 10, 50–51,

    74–75, 86

target heart rate, 10

teeth, injury to, 81

tendinitis, 68, 75–76

tendons, 2, 11, 14, 30, 32

    definition of, 68

    injury to, 75–76

tennis, 11, 16, 34, 74, 83

tennis elbow, 76–77

testosterone, 15, 100, 102

THC (delta-9

    tetrahydrocannabinol), 99

thighs, 15, 58, 72–73

    See also hamstrings

throwing, 13, 74–77

tobacco, 96–97

toes, injury to, 61–62, 84–86

track. *See* running

training

    ancient Greece, vii

    endurance, 4, 14

    excessive, 66

    heart rate, 10

    interval, 10

    log, 50–51

    muscle size and, 15

strength (progressive resistance
  training), 4, 14–16
triceps, 12, 13
turf toe, 62

ultraviolet radiation, 89, 91
underwear, 56
urine, 20, 95

vitamins, 24, 27–28
  definition of, 18
  in diet, 17, 19
volleyball, 16

walking, 10, 34, 64, 70
warm-up, 5, 29–33
  importance of, 29–30, 67–68, 75
  sport-specific, 32–33
  steps of, 31–33
water, 25–26, 88, 90–92
weather, effects of
  cold, 84–87
  hot, 87–92
weight control, 2, 5–6, 25–26, 48
weight lifting, vii, 2, 4, 10, 12,
  14–16, 34, 102
winning and losing, 49–50
wrestling, vii, 5, 79
wrists, injury to, 77–78